THE NEW TAO
of
WARREN BUFFETT

THE NEW TAO
of
WARREN BUFFETT

*Wisdom from Warren Buffett
to Help Guide You to Wealth and Make the Best
Decisions About Life and Money*

MARY BUFFETT *and* DAVID CLARK

**SIMON &
SCHUSTER**

London · New York · Sydney · Toronto · New Delhi

First published in the United States by Scribner, an imprint of Simon & Schuster, LLC, 2024
First published in Great Britain by Simon & Schuster UK Ltd, 2024

1 3 5 7 9 10 8 6 4 2

Simon & Schuster UK Ltd
1st Floor
222 Gray's Inn Road
London WC1X 8HB

Simon & Schuster: Celebrating 100 Years of Publishing in 2024

www.simonandschuster.co.uk
www.simonandschuster.com.au
www.simonandschuster.co.in

Simon & Schuster Australia, Sydney
Simon & Schuster India, New Delhi

A CIP catalogue record for this book
is available from the British Library

Hardback ISBN: 978-1-3985-4002-6
eBook ISBN: 978-1-3985-4003-3

Printed and Bound in the UK using 100% Renewable
Electricity at CPI Group (UK) Ltd

MIX
Paper | Supporting
responsible forestry
FSC® C171272
www.fsc.org

For Charlie Munger

1924–2023

"Nothing beats having a great partner . . . Charlie and I think pretty much alike. But what it takes me a page to explain, he sums up in a sentence. And his version, moreover, is always more clearly reasoned and also more artfully—some might add bluntly—stated."

—*Warren Buffett*

"You have to keep learning if you want to become a great investor, when the world changes, you have to change."

—*Charlie Munger*[1]

Contents

✳

Note to the Reader

✳

The wisdom of Warren Buffett contained in this book will open the door to discovering the investment methodology Warren used to increase the power of compounding, and in the process, obtain vastly superior long-term investment results. Once you see the light, it will shock you in its effectiveness and ease in application—that it can be done, as Warren says, with average intelligence, a willingness to read, and by simply learning to control one's emotions.

CHAPTER ONE

Warren Buffett on Making Money and Keeping Money

No. 1

"People would be better off if they say I bought a business today, instead of saying I bought a stock today."[1]

✳

At the end of the day, owning a stock is really just owning a piece of a business. A company's ownership interests are broken down into shares. If the company has 100,000 shares outstanding and you buy 10,000 of those shares, you effectively own 10% of that business. How well that company does over the long term will ultimately determine how well you do owning the stock of that business.

Warren offers the following advice to help us think about stocks being a business: *"If you're going to buy a stock . . . take a yellow pad out and write down the number of shares outstanding, multiply it by the price per stock, which will give you the market value of XX. Then ask yourself—if I had that amount of money would I spend it on buying that business? If your answer is no, then you shouldn't even be buying a single share of that company."*

No. 2

*"Do not take yearly results too seriously.
Instead, focus on four- or five-year averages."*[2]

✳

A company's net earnings for any given single year can give you an incomplete picture of what is really going on. Sometimes the picture is too rosy—other times too negative. Warren looks at the company's earnings for a four- or five-year period. He's looking for stability—with an upward trend. A company may have an off year earnings-wise. Which will turn shortsighted investors off. That will drive the stock down. If what drove the stock down is a onetime event, it potentially creates an opportunity for the investor. On the other hand, there can be a one-year spike in earnings that will make it look like the company is doing better than it actually is, which could entice the unsuspecting investor into believing a slowly dying business has turned around when it hasn't.

No. 3

*"Change is not what gives you opportunities. What gives
you opportunities is other people doing dumb things . . .
And I'd say that over the fifty-eight years we have been
running Berkshire there has been an ever-increasing number
of people doing dumb things."*[3]

❋

Dumb things occur when the shortsightedness of the stock market misprices a company from a long-term economic perspective. Meaning that people get caught up in the moment and ignore the long-term economic advantages of the business. Just listen to the quarterly investors' call most large companies have—the entire focus is on how well the company will do in the next quarter—with not a word mentioned as to the long-term prospects of the business.

There is a Wall Street maxim that "change"—new transformative technologies—will give rise to new investment opportunities— which is true—but that doesn't mean those opportunities will end up making you money. According to a 2012 study of the "Internet Boom Years" by the Kauffman Foundation, there were an estimated 400,000 new internet businesses started in the United States between 1995 and 1999. Of those, an estimated 70% went bust within five years. Start-ups will always be a risky business, no matter what the industry.

No. 4

"The real test of whether you're investing from a value standpoint or not—is if you care about whether the stock market is open tomorrow. If you're making a good investment, it shouldn't bother you if they closed down the stock market for five years."[4]

✳

Warren used to get together every other year with a group of investors, who had also studied with Benjamin Graham at Columbia University, and talk about the stock market. A question they liked to ask each other every time they met was this: If you had to go away to a deserted island for ten years, and had to put all your money in just one stock, and leave it there for those ten years, what stock would it be? And why?

Warren's answer in 1982 was Capital Cities Communications—a company that owned TV and radio stations, run by the highly talented CEO Tom Murphy. Warren's reasoning: Tom was a great manager, tight with money, and the company earned high returns on equity and had the best profit margins in the TV broadcasting business.

In March of 1985 Murphy merged Capital Cities with the television media giant ABC. Warren bought 20 million shares in the newly merged entity for $517 million to help Murphy finance the deal. Ten years later, in July 1995, Murphy sold Capital Cities/ABC to Disney for $19 billion, with Warren receiving $2.46 billion in cash and Disney stock for his 20 million shares. This gave Warren a pretax profit of $1.88 billion on his original investment, and a pretax average annual compounding rate of return of 16.8% for the ten years he held his Capital Cities/ABC stock.

No. 5

*"You've got to understand accounting.
You've got to. It's got to be like a language to you."*[5]

For Warren, accounting is the language of business—it has the power to unlock the true story behind a company's financial health. It allows him to decipher a company's financial statement—the income statement and balance sheet—and create a clear and concise narrative for the business. The financial statement will help him figure out if the company has a durable competitive advantage and what its intrinsic value is relative to the price of its stock—whether its stock is a bargain or if it's overpriced. To be a successful investor at Warren's level you absolutely need to be fluent in the language of accounting.

Please note: If you haven't had a course on accounting, we wrote a very simple—easy to understand—book for investors on how Warren uses accounting to interpret a company's financial statements. It's called *Warren Buffett and the Interpretation of Financial Statements.*

No. 6

"People basically have three options, short-term cash, which is an option for doing something later on, long-term bonds, and long-term stocks. And stocks are cheaper than bonds."[6]

✳

Cash: Holding cash is usually a horrible investment because inflation slowly erodes your purchasing power, so every day your cash is arguably worth less and less. This loss can be offset by what the cash will earn in interest sitting in short-term CDs and US Treasuries or a bank account or a money market fund. For Warren cash is a store of value, waiting to be deployed into a business at the right price. If Warren can't find the right price, he'll sit on cash, all invested in short-term US Treasuries. Why short-term? Because if he held long-term Treasuries, and interest rates jump up, the long-term Treasuries would drop in value. This is what happened to Silicon Valley Bank— the bank bought long-term Treasuries and interest rates went up. The long-term Treasuries lost so much value the bank became insolvent.

Bonds: Rising interest rates is one of the problems of holding long-term bonds. The other is that you're locked into a low interest rate for ten, twenty, thirty years, depending on the maturity of the bond. Warren put it this way: *"If you buy a thirty-year bond today with a yield of 2%, you are paying fifty times earnings, for an investment where the earnings can't go up for thirty years. Now, if somebody said I want to sell you a stock where the earnings can't go up for thirty years, you wouldn't think it's a very good investment."* Why? If inflation is running at 5% a year, you are arguably losing 3% a year on your investment ($5\% - 2\% = 3\%$).

Stocks: This is where it gets interesting. Warren realized that some businesses have exceptional economics working in their favor that will cause the company's intrinsic value to increase over time. The common stock of these amazing companies can be viewed as a kind of equity bond that has an increasing rate of interest (earnings) attached to it. When Berkshire started buying Coca-Cola stock in 1988 (adjusted for splits) it had earnings of $0.18 a share and was growing its per share earnings at a rate of approximately 15% a year. Berkshire paid approximately $3.24 a share, which equated to a P/E ratio of 18, way too high for the likes of Benjamin Graham—the Dean of Wall Street and Warren's early mentor. But Warren could see something that Graham couldn't: the long-term economics of the business made it a bargain at a P/E of 18. He recognized Coca-Cola's stock/equity as a kind of bond, which was paying an initial rate of return of 5.55% ($0.18 ÷ $3.24 = 5.55%), which would continue to increase as Coke's per share earnings continued to grow by a combination of increased sales, share buybacks, and general inflation. And that, over several years, the stock market would continue to advance Coke's share price, as the company's per share earnings continued to grow.

So how did Warren's investment in Coca-Cola do? He invested $1.3 billion in Coke in 1988. Over the last thirty-six years (2024), his investment has grown to be worth $24.4 billion, and that doesn't even include all the dividends it received over the last thirty-six years. From a dividend perspective, in 1989, Coca-Cola paid Berkshire $31 million in dividends; by 2024 Coca-Cola had grown its dividend payout to Berkshire to $736 million a year. Over the last thirty-six years Coca-Cola has paid to Berkshire a total of $11.5 billion in dividends. Giving Warren a total return of $35.9 billion, which equates to a 2,661% total return on his original 1988 investment. Things really do go better with a Coke, including Warren's money.

No. 7

"Stocks are going to outperform the 30-year Treasury bond, and they're going to outperform Treasury bills. They're going to outperform that money you stuck under your mattress."[7]

✳

The S&P 500 index—which represents 500 of the top publicly traded companies in America—turned in an average annual rate of return of 11.2% for the last ten years. For the last twenty years the S&P 500 has turned in an average annual performance of 9%. In 2024 the thirty-year Treasury bond pays an annual rate of return of 4.37%; the one-year Treasury bill pays 5%; and on the cash stuck under your mattress—nothing.

Warren believes that if you don't know what you are doing when it comes to investments, then you are much better off investing in an S&P 500 ETF (exchange-traded fund). In fact, in Warren's will he has directed his trustee to invest 90% of his wife's inheritance in a low-cost S&P 500 ETF and the remaining 10% in short-term government bonds. You can buy an S&P 500 ETF through any online brokerage firm.

No. 8

"The best thing to do if you've got a wonderful private business is just keep it. It's going to be worth more next year and the year after. So, there's no reason to sell a wonderful business except for some kind of extraneous factors."[8]

✴

This same thing can be said if you, as an individual investor, own shares in a wonderful publicly traded company with a durable competitive advantage. The underlying business of Coca-Cola, Apple, and American Express is going to be worth more next year and the year after. Their stock price might gyrate with all kinds of stock market mania, but the underlying value of these businesses will continue to grow. If you buy into these companies in a down market, at a bargain price, you are good to go for the long ride. It's how many of the early investors in Berkshire ended up billionaires—it took them fifty years to get there—but the multimillionaires started popping up after just ten years.

There are times when one has to sell their ownership interests in one of these wonderful businesses—kids have to go to college—you want to buy a beach house—inheritance taxes have to be paid. With a privately held company, it might be that there is no family member to follow in the owner/manager's footsteps, or after five generations of ownership there are dozens of owners who aren't working in the company and simply want to cash out. Whatever the reason, one should never sell a wonderful private business so you can go invest in a not-so-wonderful publicly traded one. Which—believe it or not—happens all the time.

No. 9

*"I don't advocate extreme frugality. I mean, there are
choices and there are advantages to spending money
for your family when it's young and giving them various
forms of enjoyment or education."*[9]

※

The cult of "Warren & Charlie" is a cost-conscious crowd, as are its two heroes. But some in the cult go to such extremes that they deny themselves and their families some of the great joys of having money. One has to live under one's means in order to save, but whether you live another 5% or 10% under your means every year is not going to make that much difference in the size of your pot of gold at the end of your rainbow. But the joy you have had with your family and the education you give your kids will bring you smiles to the end of your days. So, take the kids to Disneyland, live in a nice house that is within your means, and invest in your children's education; all three will pay big dividends for many years to come.

But as you travel through life, just keep in the back of your mind this cost-conscious quote that is often attributed to Charlie: *"The cheaper coach seats on a plane always arrive at the same time as the first-class seats."*

No. 10

"I try to invest in businesses that are so wonderful that an idiot can run them. Because sooner or later, one will."[10]

·※·

Warren's wonderful, idiotproof business is a company with a durable competitive advantage, which has underlying economics so good that even a moron manager can run it and get great results. What usually makes these super businesses idiotproof is that the company has been making the same products or providing the same services for the last hundred years.

Here are some of the "hundred years" idiotproof companies in which Warren has made big investments in the past: Coca-Cola Company, Wells Fargo Bank, American Express, Bank of America, Swiss Re, Wrigley's Gum, Kraft Foods, Moody's, BNSF Railway, and Mitsubishi Corporation—all of which have been selling the same products or providing the same services for the last hundred years! Warren subscribes to the "three generations rule"—if three generations of your family have been buying the same product or service, the odds are very good that the next three generations of your family will as well. The Nabisco Oreo cookie is over a hundred years old, and a hundred years from today, a glass of milk and an Oreo cookie will still be putting a smile on children's faces all over the world.

No. 11

"There is always trouble coming." [11]

※

And trouble to Warren means opportunity. But he has a very unique view. Other investors are attempting to predict when the trouble will happen. Warren is just waiting for it to happen, so he can take advantage of the lower stock prices. He might have to wait several years between "trouble"-created buying opportunities. This is where the "temperament" and "patience" come into play—you need the "temperament" to be "patient" enough to be able to wait for the "trouble" to show up. Trouble does eventually show up, and with it, lower stock prices. Sometimes the trouble brings down the stock prices of even the best of companies. Here are just a few of the really big "trouble" events in the last forty years that killed stock prices and presented Warren with potential buying opportunities:

1. **Black Monday (October 19, 1987):** The Dow Jones Industrial Average (DJIA) plunged 22.6%, the largest single-day percentage decline in its history. The crash was triggered by a combination of factors, including program trading, rising interest rates, and fears of inflation.
2. **Gulf War (1990–1991):** Kuwait was invaded by Iraq in 1990, which disrupted the oil market, sending oil prices upward and setting off fears of a global recession. The DJIA fell 17% between July and October 1990.
3. **Dot-com bubble burst (2000–2002):** The dot-com bubble was caused by excessive speculation in technology stocks. When it burst it caused a 78% decline in the Nasdaq Composite Index between March 2000 and October 2002.

4 **September 11 attacks (2001):** When al-Qaeda attacked the Twin Towers in NYC on September 11, 2001, there was an immediate decline in the stock market—the DJIA falling 14% in one week.

5 **Housing market crash (2007–2009):** An overheated housing market, fueled by subprime mortgages and loose lending practices, caused homeowners to start to default on their mortgages. The defaults negatively impacted several trillion dollars in mortgage bonds, which led to the worst stock market crash since the Great Depression. The DJIA fell 54% between October 2007 and March 2009.

6 **Lehman Brothers collapse (September 15, 2008):** The 158-year-old Wall Street investment bank Lehman Brothers, as a result of defaulting on mortgage bonds, filed for bankruptcy, which led to panic in the entire global financial system.

7 **European sovereign debt crisis (2010–2012):** Fears that Greece would default on its sovereign debt led to a decline in the European stock market.

8 **Japan earthquake and tsunami (2011):** The devastating earthquake and tsunami in Japan destroyed coastlines and severely damaged nuclear power plants, which caused a panic in the Japanese stock market.

9 **Brexit (2016):** The United Kingdom leaving the European Union caused a decline in the exchange value of the British pound and a sell-off in stock markets around the world.

10 **COVID-19 pandemic (2020):** The global pandemic caused worldwide shutdowns and economic uncertainty, which led to a stock market crash in March 2020, when the S&P 500 fell nearly 34%.

No. 12

"The best thing that happens to us is when a great company gets into temporary trouble . . . We want to buy them when they're on the operating table."[12]

✳

One of the first companies that Warren bought that was having temporary troubles was Berkshire Hathaway itself. Berkshire's textile business was experiencing a cyclical recession (Warren considers a cyclical recession to be a temporary problem), and Berkshire's stock was in the doldrums, trading at $12.50 a share vs. a per share book value of $19. Warren bought Berkshire stock as an undervalue play, with the initial intention of selling it when Berkshire came out of the cyclical recession. Instead, he ended up buying enough Berkshire stock to take control of the company, and then used the company's working capital to buy far more profitable businesses.

Similar "temporary trouble" buying opportunities played out with Warren's purchases of American Express during its salad oil scandal in 1963 (which involved executives at Allied Crude Vegetable Oil Company using fake collateral in a loan from American Express); with GEICO in 1976, when it almost went into insolvency; with R. J. Reynolds Industries (the tobacco company) in 1982, when it experienced trouble over government regulation, lawsuits, and a recession; and Coca-Cola in 1988, when it suffered decline in its stock price due to the New Coke debacle (the company tried to change the flavor of Coke) and the "Black Monday" stock market sell-off (Warren considers market "panic" sell-offs as a temporary problem). So, whenever you see some great business experiencing "a temporary problem" that is killing its stock price, you can bet you'll also find Warren sniffing around for a bargain buy.

No. 13

"It's an easy game, if you can control your emotions. If you're a young investor, and you can sort of stand back and value stocks as businesses and invest when things are very cheap, no matter what anybody is saying, and perhaps, if you wish, sell when people get terribly enthused, it is really not a very tough intellectual game."[13]

✳

We really like this quote because it sums up exactly what Warren is doing and why he is so successful. Learn how to value businesses. Ignore the news on the economy. Buy when investors are pessimistic, and things are cheap. And sell them, if you wish, when people become enthusiastic about stocks again. Learning to control your emotions is a process that takes time. To repeat Warren's favorite mantra one more time: *"Be fearful when others are greedy, and greedy when others are fearful.*

Warren Buffett on the Importance of a Company with a Durable Competitive Advantage

No. 14

"I was originally taught by Graham to invest in companies that were quantitively cheap—I call it a cigar butt approach to buying stocks—you walk down the street looking for used cigar butts that have a few puffs left in them. I did that for years—it was a mistake . . . It's much easier to make money buying a wonderful business at a fair price than a fair business at a wonderful price."[1]

✳

Benjamin Graham taught Warren to put a value on a company, and to buy it if it was selling at a discount to that value. Graham called the "discount" his "margin of safety"—he believed it protected him from loss. Once the company rose to its "intrinsic value," Graham would sell it. And if it didn't rise in value within three years, he would sell it anyway. Graham made no call on the long-term economics of the business. He wasn't interested.

In the bull market of the late 1960s these kinds of Graham "value" plays started drying up. It was during this time that Warren, with the help of Charlie, started realizing that certain companies possessed a "long-term durable competitive advantage" that created a kind of "perpetual growth in value" that made their owners fabulously wealthy the longer they held the stock. These companies never sell at prices that Graham would have found alluring, but they do occasionally sell in bear markets at prices that Warren considers fair, given their excellent long-term economics.

No. 15

"The products or services that have wide, sustainable moats around them are the ones that deliver rewards to investors."[2]

✳

Warren went through a sort of evolution in his efforts to describe the economic nature of the "excellent business." In his early days he described these as businesses that had a "consumer monopoly," meaning that when consumers wanted that kind of product or service they only thought of that company. Then he started to describe them as "businesses that owned a piece of the consumer's mind," again referring to thinking of a particular product or service when the need arose. He'd say "Disney" owns a piece of the consumers' minds.

Later, Warren explained an excellent business as being one with products or services that had a "wide, sustainable moat around them," meaning that a brand name and the underlying economics of the business protected the company from competitors. And finally, he used the phrase a company with a "durable competitive advantage" to explain what an excellent business looks like. The "durable competitive advantage" is the wide moat. The trick is to be able to identify a company with a durable competitive advantage, and then buy it at a price that makes business sense. It's a two-part equation. (We discuss Warren's methods for valuing a business later, in chapters five, ten, and eighteen.)

No. 16

"The key to investing is not assessing how much an industry is going to affect society, or how much it will grow, but rather determining the competitive advantage of any given company and, above all, the durability of that advantage."[3]

✳

In Warren's world, having a "competitive advantage" means having some economic advantage your competitors don't have. Being "durable" means that the business has staying power and is not susceptible to erosion by competition.

Companies with a "durable competitive advantage" come in an assortment of flavors: (1) There are companies that provide "unique services" and create a kind of brand loyalty that makes it hard to compete with them. Examples would be Amazon, Google, American Express, and eBay. (2) Companies that are the "low-cost seller"—these are usually "volume sellers." They have lower operating costs, which allow them to charge cheaper prices and still maintain their profit margins. The cheaper prices create customer loyalty—in the way of returning customers, who generate lots of "sales volume." Examples would be the retail giants Costco and Nebraska Furniture Mart. (3) Companies with "strong brands"—products that create customer loyalty that makes it very difficult for a competitor to enter their market. Warren thinks of a recognizable brand name as owning a piece of the consumer's mind. Coca-Cola and Apple are two perfect examples of this phenomenon.

Coke sells a product that hasn't really changed at all since it was first sold in 1886. It has 46% of the entire American soft drink market and 17% of the world soft drink market. Its 138-year history and strong market position are good indicators that Coca-Cola owns a piece of the consumers' minds and has a durable competitive advantage.

Since 2007 Apple has been selling a consumer product—the iPhone—that it is constantly improving, and that people have made an indispensable part of their lives. They talk on iPhones, send messages on them, use them to take pictures and movies, use them to get directions, use them to find out the weather forecast, use them as a wallet, use them to do banking, read a book, buy concert and movie tickets, even find their kids when they are lost. Apple iPhones connect each and every one of us to an infinite amount of knowledge stored on the internet. Not only does the name Apple iPhone own a piece of our minds, each of the individual apps on the iPhone owns a piece of the consumers' minds. After only seventeen years, Apple has 56% of the American smartphone market and 17% of the world market. Apple's iPhone's market penetration and seventeen-year history are very good indicators that the company has a durable competitive advantage with the iPhone.

Once you've identified a "brand name" that owns a piece of a consumer's mind, you need to look at the company's financials. Are their net earnings consistent and/or on an upward trend? Do they get high returns on equity? Do they carry low amounts of debt? Do they buy back their stock? All these financial metrics are characteristics of companies with a durable competitive advantage, which are the kinds of companies Warren likes to invest in. But Warren will only invest in them if they are selling at a price that makes sense to him from the perspective of buying the entire business.

No. 17

"What we want is a business with a durable competitive advantage, we want a business we understand, and we want a management that we like and trust. And then we want a price that makes sense."[4]

✳

To Warren, a business with a "competitive advantage" over its competitors means freedom to raise prices, which increases profit margins, which increases net profits, which increases the value of the business. The "durable" component has to do with having a competitive advantage that just keeps going on and on—think Coca-Cola being in business for over a hundred years. A business we "understand" means Warren understands the nature of the business, which allows him to understand the financials—which helps him figure out if the company has a durable competitive advantage working in its favor. Then Warren has to like and trust the management, because at the end of the day he is trusting them with "his" money. And finally, there is the matter of price, it has to make business "sense," and that is where people often screw up Warren's equation. It may be a company with a durable competitive advantage, in a business he understands, with management he trusts, but if he can't buy it at a price that makes sense to him from a business perspective. He isn't interested, and you shouldn't be either.

No. 18

"There are some pretty good moats around. Being the low-cost producer, for example, is a terribly important moat."[5]

✳

Not all companies with a durable competitive advantage "moat" have brand-name products driving their underlying economics; some are simply the low-cost producer in what is otherwise a highly competitive market. Being a low-cost producer is what ensures them a larger profit margin than their competitors—which means they bring more money to the bottom line. Some of the low-cost producers that Berkshire owns: The GEICO insurance company—is a low-cost producer because it sells directly to customers; it doesn't have to pay agents to sell its insurance. The BNSF Railway—has a low-cost advantage on long hauls compared to trucks, which makes it cheaper to ship by rail than by truck. The Nebraska Furniture Mart—is a low-cost producer because it owns its warehouses and retail buildings, so it doesn't have to pay rent, which means it has lower fixed costs than its competitors. Fruit of the Loom—by utilizing automation and optimizing its supply chain, it maintains its position as a low-cost producer in the mid-market underwear game.

No. 19

"I wouldn't think of the credit card business as a one-model business any more than I would think of the car business as essentially being one model. I mean, Ferrari is going to make a lot of money, but they're going to have just a portion of the market."[6]

✳

What we want you to see here is that the phenomenon of a durable competitive advantage can occur *in a segment* of a particular market. American Express went after the high end of the credit card market, being both a card issuer and a payment network. They can charge a cardholder an annual fee, and they can charge the merchant a fee. Visa and Mastercard—while phenomenally profitable—are primary payment networks. All three make lots of money. But it was American Express that developed a durable competitive advantage by going after the premium user segment of the market—and offering services like free access to exclusive airline lounges, free upgrades at five-star hotels, free travel insurance, offices in 140 different countries, and overnight lost card replacement.

Another phenomenon that influenced Warren's purchase of American Express is stock repurchases. In the period of 1993 to 1995 Warren accumulated 10% of American Express's outstanding shares for $1.392 billion. He has never spent another dime on it. Yet, through the process of American Express buying back its shares over the last twenty-nine years, Berkshire's ownership interest in the company has increased from 10% in 1995 to 20% in 2024. And that 20% has grown to be worth approximately $32.4 billion, and is producing $362 million a year in dividends. American Express, instead of going out and spending its retained earnings on iffy high-priced acquisitions, has been buying back its own stock and making its shareholders, including Warren, even richer.

CHAPTER THREE

Warren Buffett's Basic Investment Principles

No. 20

"If you're smart, you don't need a lot of money. And if you're dumb, no amount of money is going to help you."[1]

*

If you're smart you will understand the power of compounding interest. You will know the difference between a company that has a durable competitive advantage and one that doesn't. And you will know how to value a company to determine if it is overpriced or underpriced. With that knowledge you can take even a small sum of money and grow it exponentially to be worth millions of dollars. But if you're dumb, even if you start with millions, eventually you are going to lose it all.

No. 21

*"The important thing is to know what you know
and know what you don't know."*[2]

＊

The secret behind Warren's incredible success is not an incredible intellect or being the all-knowing oracle of Omaha. In fact, it's just the opposite. It's actually about knowing what he doesn't know. This stops Warren from making investment decisions he isn't qualified to make.

An accountant would be inviting folly if he tried to play doctor. Warren feels the same way about investing. There are certain companies he has no idea how to value, and as a result he stays away from them. Then there are companies that he understands and feels very qualified to value—these are the ones that have made him super rich.

Warren refers to this world of businesses that he understands well enough to value as his "circle of competence"—which means he is confident in his ability to value them. If he can confidently value companies, he can confidently tell if the stock market is undervaluing them or overvaluing them. For Warren, being able to spot when the market is undervaluing a company shows him where the big money is.

No. 22

*"Don't save what is left after spending;
spend what is left after saving."*[3]

＊

One gets rich by getting their money to work for them, but that
won't happen unless they first have money saved up to make that
initial investment. For most people the first money they have to
invest comes from saving a percentage of what they earn from a job.

In Warren's teenage days he was obsessed with saving money
from the various little businesses he ran. And with his obsession
for saving money came an aversion to spending it. Warren was so
averse to spending money that he drove an old Volkswagen Beetle
long after he had become a multimillionaire, and he still lives in the
same house he paid $31,500 for in 1957. In Warren's case, saving
money was way more fun than spending money, unless, of course,
he was buying stocks.

No. 23

"My wealth has come from a combination of living in America, some lucky genes, and compound interest."[4]

✳

Albert Einstein—the genius physicist—once said, "Compound interest is the eighth wonder of the world. He who understands it earns it . . . He who doesn't, pays it." Warren took this to heart early in his life and it truly has been the gift that kept on giving.

Here is how compounding interest works: $50,000 compounding at 10% a year will be worth $55,000 after one year, $60,500 after two years, $66,550 after three years. After ten years it will be worth $129,687. After twenty years it will be worth $336,375. After thirty years, $872,470. After forty years, $2,262,962. After fifty years, $5,869,542.

In the first ten years we made $79,687 in interest on our $50,000 investment. But between the years ten and twenty we made $206,688 in interest. And between years twenty to thirty we made $536,095 in interest. Between the years thirty and forty we made $1,390,492 in interest. Between the years forty and fifty we made $3,606,580 in interest. As the pot gets bigger, we make more and more in interest, which grows the pot even larger.

When Warren took over Berkshire Hathaway, he stopped the company from paying a dividend so all the earnings would build up in Berkshire. Using his investment prowess, Warren got Berkshire's shareholders' equity to compound at the phenomenal rate of 18.55% a year for fifty-nine years, growing shareholder's equity from $24.5 million in 1965 to approximately $561.2 billion in 2024, for a total gain of 2,290,512%. Responding to the increase in shareholder's equity, the market price for Berkshire's stock, from 1965 to 2024, grew from $12.50 a Class A share to $632,000 a Class A share, which equates to an annual compounding growth rate of approximately 20.15%.

Note: Our $50,000 investment compounding at a rate of 20.15% a year, for fifty-nine years, would be worth $2.52 billion in year fifty-nine, which is exactly how several of Warren's early investors ended up billionaires.

No. 24

"From the standpoint of investments, you need two courses in a business school: one is how to value a business, and the other is how to think about stock market fluctuations."[5]

✳

If Warren was teaching a course in business school on how to value a business, he would teach students that there are basically two kinds of businesses: (1) Businesses that sell commodity-type products, which have lots of price competition, low profit margins, low returns on equity, and volatile net earnings. These are the companies you don't want to own. (2) Exceptional businesses, which have some kind of durable competitive advantage, as evidenced by little price competition, high profit margins, high returns on equity, consistent earnings, and are buying back their shares. These are the right companies to own, and once identified, Warren would explain to the students how to tell if they are selling at a price that makes business sense to buy them.

Warren's course on stock market fluctuations would provide a historical study of what market forces create buying opportunities. He would teach the students the history of events and forces that dramatically affect stock prices, what drives them from insane highs to depressing lows, and how these events can affect the stock prices of companies with a durable competitive advantage and in the process create investment opportunities.

No. 25

*"You don't want to be a no emotion person in all of your life,
but you definitely want to be a no emotion person in making
an investment or business decision."*[6]

※

Warren's investment decisions—after weighing the economics of the business and the price he is paying—are based solely on whether or not he believes he is getting good value for his money. He's very cold about it. In his early days, if he had a position that was making him money, even if he loved the company, if something better came along, he would sell it in a nanosecond and go with the new prospect. He bought and sold his favorite Capital Cities Communications several times before he settled into a long-term position with it. This is the reason Warren doesn't react with fear in a stock market panic. His lack of emotion enables him to see long-term value and buy when everyone else is running for the fire escape. It's also why he doesn't get caught up in the euphoria of a bull market and end up paying insane prices for businesses.

No. 26

"The most important item over time in valuation is obviously interest rates. If interest rates are destined to be at very low levels... it makes any stream of earnings from investments worth more money."[7]

✳

Let's say that Company A constantly produces earnings of $10 million a year. In a world of 10% interest rates, we would have to invest $100 million in bonds that were paying 10% to earn $10 million a year. Warren would argue that Company A is worth $100 million relative to a 10% interest rate. ($100 million × 10% = $10 million.)

Now, let's say interest rates dropped to 2%. We would have to invest $500 million in bonds paying 2% to earn $10 million a year. ($500 million × 2% = $10 million.) Warren would argue that Company A's earnings of $10 million a year are now worth $500 million relative to the 2% interest rate.

The same inverse relationship also exists when discounting the future cash flows of a business to present value. The higher the discount rate, the lower the present value. The lower the discount rate, the higher the present value. So, a payment of $10 million a year for ten years, discounted to present value, using a rate of 10%, would have a present value of $61.3 million. But if we used a 2% discount rate, a payment of $10 million a year for ten years would have a present value of $89.4 million.

When interest rates drop, the relative value of what businesses earn goes up—and eventually stock prices will follow upward as well. But when interest rates go up, the relative value of what businesses earn goes down—and stock prices will eventually go down as well.

No. 27

"Obviously, profits are worth a whole lot more if the government bond yield is 1 percent than they're worth if the government bond yield is 5 percent."[8]

✳

For Warren, all investment valuations are invariably linked to interest rates. If you owned a share of Apple stock and it earned $6.43 a share in 2023, you would need $128 invested in a 5% government bond to yield you $6.43. But in a world of 1% government bonds, you would need $643 invested in 1% government bonds to yield $6.43. So as interest rates go down, stock prices "tend" to go up. And if interest rates go up, stock prices "tend" to go down. Why government bonds? If they are United States Treasury bonds, they are thought of as being risk free of default. In 2024 ten-year U.S. Treasury Bonds traded at 4.3%, which gave Apple's $6.43 a share earnings a relative value of $149 a share, against Apple shares reaching an all-time trading high in 2024 of $225 a share, which was 66% above its relative value of $149 a share. Warren's response to this overvaluation was to start selling his holdings in Apple. Even the best of companies can become overvalued—and when they do Warren will often cut his position.

No. 28

"We do like having a lot of money to be able to operate very fast and very big. We know we won't get those opportunities frequently . . . In the next 20 or 30 years there'll be two or three times when it'll be raining gold and all you have to do is go outside. But we don't know when they will happen. And we have a lot of money to commit."[9]

✳

Charlie used to put it like this: *"You have to be very patient. You have to wait until something comes along, which, at the price you're paying, is easy. That's contrary to human nature, just to sit there all day long doing nothing, waiting. It's easy for us, we have a lot of other things to do. But for an ordinary person, can you imagine just sitting for five years doing nothing? You don't feel active, you don't feel useful, so you do something stupid."* This is not the investment strategy of any fund manager in the world. Hold billions in cash and wait for the world to fall apart. But it is true, every ten years or so the financial world does fall apart and stock prices tank across the board. It happened in 2000 when the internet bubble burst, it happened in 2008 to 2009 when Wall Street imploded with the mortgage backed bonds, it happened in 2020 with the COVID shut down, and it will happen again, and again. And when it happens stock prices will collapse, and the Federal Reserve banks of the world will do what they always do, which is print tons of cash to pull us out of it, which will ultimately be bullish for stock prices. The hedge funds, mutual funds, and investment trusts of the world can't play Warren's waiting game, they can't sit on cash waiting for the mega opportunity. But Warren can. And so can you!

No. 29

*"Opportunities come infrequently. When it rains gold,
put out the bucket, not the thimble."* [10]

＊

Warren often talks about temperament. He means having the
patience to wait for the right opportunity. By his own admission
he has sometimes sat waiting patiently for several years for the right
investment opportunity to show up. And when it finally shows up,
he takes full advantage and buys big.

Back in the 1980s, Warren spent $1.3 billion on Coca-Cola
stock—which, as we said, today, in 2024, is worth approximately
$24.4 billion; and in the 1990s he spent $1.4 billion on American
Express shares—which are now worth approximately $32.4 billion.
In the 2000s he bought $14 billion worth of Bank of America
stock—which was worth approximately $35.1 billion in 2024 when
he started thinning his position; and in the 2010s he spent $31 billion
for his Apple shares—which in the beginning of 2024 were worth a
whopping $176.8 billion before he started selling his position. Invest
big and win big—if you follow in Warren's footsteps and buy shares
in a company with a durable competitive advantage, and you buy it
at a price that makes sense from a business perspective.

No. 30

"There are a lot of businesses I wouldn't buy even if I thought the management was the most wonderful in the world, because they are simply in the wrong business." [11]

※

This goes back to something Warren said in the 1990s: *"When a management with a reputation for brilliance tackles a business with a reputation for poor fundamental economics, it is the reputation of the business that remains intact."* Some businesses have inherent underlying economics that are so bad that even the best managers in the world can't improve upon them. These are usually companies that sell a commodity-type product or service in which there is a lot of price competition, that historically sees a repetitive cycle of boom and bust. In the boom years demand outstrips supplies, creating huge profit margins, but in the bust years, low demand kills their profit margins, and their fixed costs end up killing them. You can easily identify these businesses by an erratic earnings history—losses some years, very profitable in other years. They never buy back their shares, and usually carry a large amount of debt. All of which tells you it's the wrong business to own—no matter what the selling price is.

CHAPTER FOUR

Warren Buffett on
Stock Market Dynamics

No. 31

"The stock market is a device for transferring money from the impatient to the patient."[1]

✳

The stock market is primarily made up of impatient, shortsighted speculators masquerading as investors. This shortsightedness causes them to buy and sell stock without any real appreciation of the long-term economics of the business. All this speculation sometimes drives stock prices to ridiculous highs, and at other times to insane lows, completely ignoring the long-term economics of the underlying business.

Warren buys when the shortsighted speculators drive the stock price down below the long-term economic value of the company. Then he patiently waits, knowing that the underlying economics of the business will eventually pull the stock price back up in alignment with its long-term economic value.

No. 32

"I have no idea where the markets are going to go tomorrow or the next day or the next month or the next year. I do know that in the end stocks tend to sell for what they are worth. At least in the range of what they are worth. They go all over the place in between—but tend to true value in the end."[2]

✳

Warren's eighty-three years of experience in buying and selling stocks has taught him that no matter how high a company's stock may go, or how low it might fall, eventually the stock will sell for its true value as a money-making enterprise. When the shortsighted stock market oversells a business relative to its underlying long-term economics, Warren knows that eventually, the market will readjust the company's stock price upward to reflect that value. And that is where he makes his money.

No. 33

*"The best times to deploy capital are
when things are going down."*[3]

＊

Warren is looking to deploy capital or buy shares when prices are going down. He patiently waits for what is called a "Black Swan" event, which is an unexpected event that causes stock prices to fall. A black swan event can happen to individual companies, to certain market segments, to entire industries, and to entire markets.

Warren started buying American Express during its 1963 "salad oil crisis," which drove the stock down. In the stock market crash of 1973 to '74, Warren bought shares in Disney and the *Washington Post*, and he bought the entire See's Candies company. In the stock market decline of 1988, Warren first started to buy shares in the Coca-Cola Company (he could see a long-term economic value the stock market couldn't see because it was too short-term focused).

During the internet boom of the late 1990s, when non-listed brick-and-mortar businesses were being sold cheap because they weren't internet companies and had limited growth potential, he bought the Nebraska Furniture Mart (a private company). When the internet bubble burst in 2000 and drove the entire market down, Warren bought into Moody's (the ratings company). In the financial crisis of 2008, which caused the financial companies to crash, he invested in Goldman Sachs. In 2009, when the market was still depressed, he bought the BNSF Railway. When the stock market experienced a decline in the last half of 2016, Warren started buying shares in Apple.

No. 34

"I know of no one that has been successful at really making a lot of money predicting the actions of the market itself. I know a lot of people who have done well picking businesses and buying them at sensible prices."[4]

*

Warren isn't a man trying to "predict" when the next Black Swan event will take the stock market down. But he is a man "waiting" for a Black Swan event to take the stock market down. They are two different things. Trying to predict when it will happen is almost impossible. Taking advantage of it when it happens is easy. One takes a fortune teller's insight to predict when something will happen in the future; the other just takes a great deal of patience waiting for the inevitable to happen. And this phenomenon can play out with individual companies at any time, in any kind of market—a one-off event kills a company's stock for a year or two—giving Warren a buying opportunity while waiting for the next black swan to swim into his life and tank the entire show!

No. 35

"We think any company that has an economist has one employee too many."[5]

❋

Warren added: *"I can't recall ever making an acquisition or turning down one based on macro-economic factors. Whether it was See's Candy, or the BNSF Railroad, we bought both at a terrible time in general economic conditions."*

People find it hard to believe that Warren does not consider macro events in the economy when it comes to buying companies or making an investment in the stock market, but he doesn't. Warren doesn't care what the inflation rate is. He doesn't care if the Federal Reserve Bank is raising rates—or cutting rates. He doesn't care about the price of oil or the current GDP of the country. What Warren focuses on is figuring out what's likely to be the average profitability of the "business" over time, how strong its competitive advantage is, and if the asking price makes business sense. Warren believes that since he is buying the business with the intention to hold it for twenty or more years, the current macroeconomic environment is of zero importance.

Charlie put it like this: *"We have made very little progress in life by trying to outguess these macroeconomic factors. We basically have abdicated. We're just swimming all the time, and we let the tide take care of itself."*

No. 36

"Remember that the stock market is manic depressive."[6]

✳

Warren's mentor, Benjamin Graham, taught him to think of the stock market as an individual named Mr. Market. Each day, Mr. Market offers you a price at which he is willing to either buy or sell shares in a business. However, Mr. Market is not a rational actor. He is driven by his emotions, swinging wildly from optimism to pessimism, regardless of the underlying economics of the business itself.

When Mr. Market is in a manic phase, he sees gold under every rock. He believes that the company's stock price will reach the moon and the time to buy is *NOW!* This is when investors are driven by euphoria, greed, and the fear of missing out. At these times, Mr. Market buys stocks at wildly inflated prices, oblivious to the potential danger of paying too much for a company. In these moments of market enthusiasm and resulting high prices Warren steps away from the market and avoids buying anything.

Then there are other periods when Mr. Market is depressed, he sees only doom and gloom. He believes that the financial world is on the brink of collapse and starts to sell stocks at rock-bottom prices. This is when investors are gripped by fear and panic, selling their shares at prices that are below the intrinsic value of the underlying businesses. This is when Warren gets excited about buying stocks.

Warren has discovered that the key to navigating this manic-depressive market lies in understanding the difference between price and value. Unlike Mr. Market, who is swayed by emotions, Warren is focused on the **intrinsic value** of a business—its long-term prospects, its durable competitive advantage. And he is focused on the price he pays. The lower the price the more interested he is in making the investment. Warren also understands that the market's depressive states don't last forever, and when Mr. Market's euphoria returns, the investments he just bought at bargain prices will soar in value.

No. 37

*"Sometimes the stock market is quite investment oriented . . .
And other times, it's almost totally a casino . . . a gambling
parlor . . . We depend on mispriced businesses through a
mechanism where we're not responsible for the mispricing of
them. And overall, we learned something a long time ago, that
it doesn't take a high IQ. It just takes the right attitude."*[7]

❋

These two statements encapsulate Warren's theory that the stock market has a massive "gambling" aspect to it that occasionally "misprices" wonderful businesses. When this happens, it is the time to buy shares in these great businesses. To do this as an investor doesn't take an enormous amount of intelligence, but rather, just the right attitude or temperament to do just the opposite of what the gamblers are doing. When the gamblers are overly enthusiastic (bull market), you store your cash, and you buy when the gamblers are panic selling and mispricing businesses (bear market). You needn't be an investment wizard to execute Warren's investment strategy—you just need the temperament to do the opposite of what the gamblers are doing. You can do this with individual companies if you're willing to do the research; or you can buy an ETF for the S&P 500 if you just want to sit back and enjoy the ride.

No. 38

"What we see when we look at the stock market is we see thousands and thousands and thousands of companies priced every day, and we ignore 99.9 percent of what we see, although we run our eyes over them. And then every now and then we see something that looks like it's attractively priced to us, as a business."[8]

❋

To Warren it's not a "stock market"—it's a "business market" where ownership interests in businesses are bought and sold. He is shopping for entire businesses, and for partial ownership interests in individual businesses.

But besides being a market where ownership interests for businesses are bought and sold, it is also a $60 trillion–plus gambling casino where enormous investment funds place multimillion-dollar-plus bets on the short-term price movements of the "shares" of these individual businesses. As an example of the enormous number of players in this casino—there are 6,559 different investment funds that are invested in Apple shares alone.

Sometimes these giant investment funds become overly optimistic about a company's short-term prospects and overprice the business relative to its underlying long-term economics. At other times these investment funds become overly pessimistic about the short-term prospects of a business and oversell its shares relative to its underlying long-term economics. It's when the investment funds become pessimistic about a company's short-term prospects and oversell its shares that Warren sometimes discovers a "wonderful business" selling at an attractive price.

No. 39

"A business that constantly encounters major change
also encounters many chances for major error. Furthermore,
economic terrain that is forever shifting violently is ground
on which it is difficult to build a fortress-like business franchise."[9]

✳

Warren goes on to add: *"Experience indicates that the best business*
returns are usually achieved by companies that are doing something they
were doing five years ago." When a company is in a business that is
constantly changing it has to spend a fortune on research and development, retooling plants and reeducating employees to stay in the
game. A Coca-Cola bottling plant will stay in production until the
machinery wears out. Not so with a silicon chip manufacturer that
has to retool every time they upgrade their chips and is constantly
faced with plant obsolescence long before the machinery has worn
out. It can take years and cost billions to retool a silicon chip plant.

Constant change is one of the big problems facing auto and
truck companies. Every new model incurs the tremendous cost of
retooling manufacturing plants. Companies that constantly change
are ones that Warren has learned to avoid.

No. 40

"Investment success depends on buying into the right businesses at the right price. And you have to know how to value businesses, and you have to have an attitude that divorces you from being influenced by the market. You want the market there, not to influence you, you want it there to serve you."[10]

✳

Letting the stock market serve you. It's an interesting concept. The stock market serves Warren by occasionally mispricing wonderful businesses that have great long-term economics working in their favor. What Warren means by the market not being there to "influence you" is for you not to get so caught up in a stock market panic that you sell everything and become afraid to buy into beaten-down companies with a durable competitive advantage. Nor do you become so caught up in a bull market buying frenzy that you end up paying insane prices for these businesses.

CHAPTER FIVE

Warren Buffett on the Right Price to Pay for a Business or Stock

No. 41

"A stock can be a good buy or a bad buy, it all depends on price."[1]

＊

What is a good buy? What's a bad buy? Depends on the price—because the price you pay will ultimately determine your rate of return.

Let us show you: Between 2016 and 2020 Warren spent roughly $31 billion buying Apple stock—at an average per share price of $34 a share and average P/E ratio of roughly 16—which bought him approximately 907 million shares of Apple stock.

But if Warren had paid Apple's high trading price in 2020 of $68 a share—or 32 times earnings—his $31 billion would've only bought him 455 million shares of Apple stock.

In the beginning of 2024 Apple's stock traded at $195 a share and Warren's 907 million shares were worth $176.8 billion—which, on his original $31 billion investment, gave him a profit of $145.8 billion and a total return of 470%.

But if he had paid the high trading price of $68 a share for his Apple stock—P/E of 32—his $31 billion would've gotten him 455 million Apple shares, which at $195 a share in 2024 would be worth $88.7 billion—which, on his original investment of $31 billion would've given him a profit of $57.7 billion and a total return of 186%.

The higher the per share price, the lower your return. The lower the per share price, the higher your return. At a P/E of 32, Warren would've taken a pass on Apple, but at a P/E of 16, it was a great buy.

No. 42

*"You can pay too much for a wonderful business . . .
You can turn any investment into a bad deal by paying
too much."*[2]

✳

A company is making $50 million a year in net profits. And it can do this year after year, which makes it a wonderful business. Now let's say we get all super excited about the business and paid 50 times earnings—$2.5 billion—for it. Our annual return on our investment will be 2% on our $2.5 billion investment. Which means, comparatively speaking, we would have been better off investing in thirty-year Treasuries that are paying a 4.37% rate of return and would earn us $109.2 million a year.

This is an example of paying too much for a wonderful business. It's still a wonderful business, it still earns $50 million a year, but at the price we paid for it, 50 times earnings—$2.5 billion—we destroyed the great underlying economics for us as buyers, thus turning a wonderful business into a bad deal.

No. 43

*"We aren't going to look at any given company
and say, 'Regardless of price, we're going to buy this,'
because we don't buy anything when the
phrase 'regardless of price' enters into the sentence."*[3]

✳

This is the price discipline that Warren lives by, and it is his key to getting really rich. The price you pay will determine your rate of return. The lower the price you pay, the higher your return will be. The higher the price you pay, the lower your rate of return will be. Companies with a durable competitive advantage are prone to becoming grossly overpriced in a bull market. Which is the wrong time to buy them. And in a bear market, companies with a durable competitive advantage can become seriously underpriced. Which is the right time to buy them.

So, save your money, make a list of fifteen companies that you identify as having a durable competitive advantage, wait for the next "panic" selling event, and then take your savings and go bargain hunting. And never buy any company "regardless of the price."

No. 44

*"So, what you really want is a business that can have
pricing that reflects inflation and does not have very much
capital investment that reflects inflation."*[4]

✳

What Warren is talking about is "pricing flexibility" in the face of
inflation, which means a business can easily adjust its prices to match
the rising cost of materials and labor. This ensures that the company's
profit margins will stay healthy despite inflationary pressures eroding
value. Companies in highly competitive markets will struggle with
this because they use price to compete with each other, which kills
their freedom to price.

Warren is also talking about a business having low ongoing
"capital investment" costs that are subject to inflationary pressures. If
a business requires constant investments in equipment, infrastructure,
or other assets, inflation will increase those costs over time, squeezing
profitability. Businesses with low ongoing capital investment needs
are in a much better positioned to handle inflationary pressures.

The perfect example of a business with pricing flexibility and
low ongoing capital investment needs is Berkshire's retail jewelry
businesses. As inflation raises salaries percentagewise, people spend
the same as they have always spent. And those diamond earrings
that once sold for $5,000 for a pair twenty years ago now sell for
$12,000 a pair. The markup on fine jewelry is high—usually 50% or
more of the asking price. When the diamond earrings cost $5,000
a pair the jewelry store makes a $2,500 profit. Now, when they cost
$12,000 a pair, the jewelry store makes a $6,000 profit. And in
the jewelry business, unlike the clothing business, there is no such

thing as product obsolescence. In fact, just the opposite occurs; those diamonds in the store's inventory actually increase in value each year. And the jewelry store has almost no capital equipment expenditures—the store's vault is a hundred years old, those jewelry cases are all fifty years old, and besides upgrading the cash registers now and then, once the store is built out, that's pretty much it. In Warren's Omaha, three generations have been buying their fine jewelry from Borsheims—owned by Berkshire—and it is completely foreseeable that the next three generations will be doing so as well.

No. 45

*"I mean, prices do amazing things in securities markets.
And when they do something that strikes us as amazing
in our direction, you know, we will act. But we do not know
today what we're going to be doing tomorrow."*[5]

✳

In the summer and fall of 2002, in the aftermath of the dot-com bust
and the 9/11 attacks, the junk bond market fell apart, and prices fell
to the point that many junk bonds were paying a 30% to 35% yield to
maturity. Warren spent $8 billion buying junk bonds in companies
he understood. Commenting on his 2002 junk bond purchases,
Warren said: *"Interestingly enough, within 12 months, some of those
same securities that were yielding 30 or 35 percent went to prices where
they yielded only 6 percent. I mean, that is truly remarkable when you
think about that happening in a country that was not in the throes of
depression or anything."* As the yield on the junk bonds went back
down, the price on the junk bonds went up. It has been reported that
Warren made as much as 30% on his $8 billion investment within
a year. Now, does this mean that Warren is a regular buyer of junk
bonds? No. It just means that when opportunity knocks on the door,
Warren will answer it in a big way.

No. 46

*"We've always wanted to acquire entire businesses.
It's just that we've found that much of the time we could
get far more for our money, in terms of wonderful
businesses, by buying pieces in the stock market, than we
could by a negotiated purchase of an entire business."*[6]

❋

Warren could've never bought the entire Coca-Cola Company at a P/E of 15, but in the 1988 bear stock market, he did buy 3.8% of the company at a P/E of 15 for $592 million. Nor could he have ever bought all of Apple at a P/E of 16, but he did buy 3.3% of the company at a P/E of 16 for $20 billion during the 2016–17 global slowdown. Warren has said repeatedly over the years that in a negotiated purchase of an entire company he has never gotten a bargain price, that the best he can hope for is a fair purchase price. But occasionally the shortsighted stock market does crazy things in a bear market that offers up small pieces of some of the world's best companies at unheard-of prices.

So why doesn't Warren just buy the entire company during the stock market sell-off? Two reasons: (1) The price on the company's shares doesn't stay low enough, long enough for Warren to acquire more of the stock at the attractive bargain price, and (2) since Warren is often spending $500 million or more buying a company's stock, he can actually help push a fallen stock price back upward, and out of his "bargain buy" price range. Those of us working with smaller amounts of money will not be plagued by these two problems.

CHAPTER SIX

Warren Buffett on Investment Advisers

No. 47

*"We believe that according the name
'investors' to institutions that trade actively
is like calling someone who repeatedly
engages in one-night stands a romantic."* [1]

✳

Okay—let's stop for a moment and really think about this: Warren has always seen the short-term trading of stocks as an invitation for folly because it is rank speculation, in which one is betting on the short-term economic winds and directional momentum of an individual stock or an entire market. It's never a sure thing. The irony is that while Warren sees its folly and advises against short-term trading, it's what creates all his investment opportunities. It has been estimated that up to 90% of all investment funds are short-term focused. Investors get in and out of stocks on every economic whim: Interest rates are going up—get out! Interest rates are going down—buy! AI is the next big thing—buy! Greece is going to default on its bonds—sell! The EU Central Bank is coming to the rescue—buy! Wall Street banks are going under—sell everything!

All this investment fund "gold rush" buying produces inflated stock prices that are often completely detached from any long-term economic reality these companies have. Panic selling does just the opposite—it can produce deflated stock prices that are a fraction of what these businesses are worth to a long-term investor like Warren. Basically, it is the short-term stock traders' panic selling that is putting a smile on Warren's face. And here is the fun part: This short-term trading "panic selling" phenomenon has been producing golden eggs for Warren for the last seventy years. And it will keep on producing golden opportunities for the next seventy years as well, because, as we said, these short-term traders (who call themselves investors) make up 90% of the market. For Warren these are the people who have made him super rich.

No. 48

"This business where somebody says, 'You should have 60% of your money in bonds and 40% in equities.' We don't go through anything like that. I mean, we regard that as nonsense."[2]

※

Investment advisers often use financial forecasts for the economy to move your money around from bond funds to stock/equity funds. They tell you, "The financial forecast is for the stock market to go down in the year ahead, so we recommend reweighting your portfolio from 70% equities and 30% bonds to 30% equities and 70% bonds." A year later they will recommend reweighting your portfolio again, and the next year they will do it again. This is one of the services they provide to justify their yearly fee. Warren regards portfolio reweighting as nonsense because he doesn't believe anyone can predict what the stock market will do in the year ahead. He does believe that over the next ten years the stock market is generally headed higher, but foreseeing its yearly ups and downs is guesswork at best.

No. 49

"Wall Street—a community in which quality control is not prized—will sell investors anything they will buy."[3]

✳

Investors want a high return with minimal risk of loss. But that is not the way the game is played. The rule of the land is the higher the return, the greater the risk of loss. But here is where Wall Street steps in—through the magic of "salesmanship" investment advisers can sell their clients on the return being "high" but the risk being "low," even when it is not. To help investment advisers do this, Wall Street investment bankers conjure up all kinds of "high reward/low risk" investment products to sell to unsuspecting customers. They like to give these investments exotic names—the Quanto and the Rainbow Option, the Constant Maturity Swap and the Bermudan Option. Then there are the Principal Protected Notes, and the Autocallable Notes, Reverse Convertibles, and the Phoenix Notes. And let's not forget the Volatility Swap and, most famous of all, the Credit Default Swap. All of which are designed to baffle the investor to the point that they will never ever understand what they just bought. Which puts them completely in the hands of their trusted Wall Street investment adviser—who tells them this magical investment offers both a high return and low risk. And just for safety's sake they will also tell the investor to diversify their portfolio to better protect them from some unforeseen calamity. It's what smart investors do.

What these Wall Street market wizards aren't telling investors is that the products they are buying are often super risky, and the reason for the diversification is to protect the investment adviser from looking like a complete idiot when one of these supersafe "investment products" crashes and burns. (In 2008 a number of these supersafe Wall Street investment products all went under at once, which not only wiped out investors, but also took down several of the big Wall Street investment banks as well.)

No. 50

"There's been far, far, far more money made by people on Wall Street through salesmanship abilities than through investment abilities."[4]

✳

The easiest sell on Wall Street is last year's investment record. The next easiest sell is the one-to-three-year track record. No one cares about the five-year record and they care even less about the ten-year record. Given that 90% of investment funds completely turn over their portfolios every one to three years, would you really expect their customers to have an even longer time frame? For the large investment houses that operate hundreds of different funds—all with different investment strategies—on any given year four or five of their funds will have done really well, which gives their sales force—brokers and investment advisers—something to "talk up" with their customers. However, the long-term investment picture may tell a different story.

No. 51

"Most professional investors focus on what the stock is likely to do in the next year. And they have all kinds of arcane methods for approaching that. They do not really think of themselves as owning a piece of a business."[5]

✳

This shortsightedness creates opportunity for Warren. Professional investors are driven to produce yearly results so they can say they have the best performing fund of the year, which then attracts more people to invest in their fund, which increases the funds they manage, which increases how much money they earn from management fees.

However, in the process of seeking short-term profits, these shortsighted professional investors often neglect to acknowledge the underlying long-term economics of the business. These investors often oversell a company because its short-term prospects don't look very good. Warren, however, will value the business from a long-term perspective, as if he were going to buy the whole company and hold it for years. If the shortsighted stock price is lower than Warren's long-term valuation, it might present a buying opportunity for him, provided the company also has some kind of durable competitive advantage in its marketplace that will ensure his long-term valuation will come to fruition.

CHAPTER SEVEN

Warren Buffett on the Investment Aspects of Inflation

No. 52

"The long term is very easy to predict in a general way, but I can't predict what the stock prices will do ten days from now or ten months from now." [1]

✳

What Warren has figured out is that the long-term price inflation caused by the government printing more and more money will eventually raise the revenue and profits of companies that possess some kind of durable competitive advantage. This is also true of an ever-increasing population, which will increase the demand for a variety of products, which will increase sales volume and profits. This is because the "demand" for these companies' products and services doesn't wane as prices increase. Companies keep their profit margins and make more and more money as rising prices and sales volume increases their revenue, which increases profits, which eventually causes the underlying business value to increase.

Think of it this way: In 1980 a house down the street from Warren's childhood home sold for $47,000 and today that same house is worth $437,000. So, who will profit from the inflation in the house's price? The realtor who sold the house in 1980 earned a commission of approximately $2,300. If it sold today, with a valuation of $437,000, the realtor would earn a commission of approximately $21,000. Then there is the insurance company. In 1980 the $47,000 house cost $400 a year to insure. Today, the same house would cost approximately $2,700 a year to insure. And then there is the bank. On a thirty-year mortgage for $47,000 at a rate of 5%, the bank would earn approximately $43,840 in interest over the thirty-year period. But if we bump that thirty-year loan up to the entire $437,000 sales price, the bank will earn approximately $407,000 in interest.

Housing inflation helps the real estate companies, the insurance companies, and the banks all earn more money. And here is the best part: Besides computer upgrades, many of these businesses don't have to keep improving their office infrastructure to increase their business; most are still in the same buildings they were in thirty years ago. Berkshire's insurance operation, The National Indemnity Company (NICO), has been in the same building since Warren bought the company in 1967. In the fifty-five years he has owned NICO, it has grown its written premiums from $19 million in 1967 to $22 billion in 2023—all from the same building, all on the same office phones, with the addition of email. And none of these businesses ever have to face product obsolescence—people will be buying houses, insurance, and borrowing money from banks a hundred years from now.

Warren found this same principle works for auto dealerships and auto insurance. As inflation causes the prices of cars to go up, the auto dealer earns more and more on each car, and the auto insurance company keeps writing larger and larger policies for more and more expensive vehicles. And more people means more cars sold and more auto insurance policies written. This is why Berkshire Hathaway owns real estate companies, property and auto insurance companies, auto dealerships, and a large position in a major bank.

Charlie put it like this: "*While we don't like inflation because it's bad for our country and our civilization, however, we will probably make more money over time because there is inflation.*"

No. 53

"Nobody wants a lot of inflation,
except a person with a lot of debt."[2]

✳

If you live in a world with 10% inflation, every year prices will rise
by 10%, and every year your purchasing power will decline by 10%.
But as inflation causes prices to rise, salaries also tend to rise. Not
always in unison, but eventually salaries do increase. The federal
minimum wage in 1960 was $1 an hour; today it is $7.25 an hour. In
1960 you would have to work 100,000 hours at $1 an hour to earn
$100,000—which equates to forty-eight years. Today, you would be
earning $7.25 an hour and it would take you 13,793 hours of work
(6.6 years) to earn that $100,000. Back in 1960, $100,000 would
buy you a mansion in the Midwest; today it might buy you a shack.
So, the trick was to borrow $100,000 in 1960, buy the mansion, and
not have to pay it off until sometime in the distant future, the further
out the better, when you can use your inflated earning power to pay
back your 1960 $100,000 loan.

But it gets even more interesting. Let's say you borrowed
$1 million today to buy a home, and you have a fixed thirty-year
mortgage at 3% and inflation is at 5%. In theory, your $1 million
house is rising in value 5% a year, but the $1 million you used to buy
it is only costing you 3%, so we can argue that you are earning 2% on
the spread between the two (5% − 3% = 2%). But if inflation jumps
to 10%, we can then argue that you are earning 7% on the spread
(10% − 3% = 7%). Earning 7% a year on $1 million equates to earn-
ing $70,000 a year in increased value. If you borrowed $10 million

and bought a $10 million home, we could argue you are earning $700,000 a year in inflation-created value. And the more inflation there is, the more you profit on the difference between your cost of the loan and the rise in the value of your property. So, according to Warren, if you are borrowing money today to buy a home, inflation becomes your new best friend.

CHAPTER EIGHT

Warren Buffett on the
Advantages of Holding Cash

No. 54

"We believe in having cash—there have been a few times in history, and there will be more times in history, where if you don't have it, you don't get to play the next day."[1]

✳

Having cash when no one else has it is a key component in Warren's investment strategy. He stumbled upon it by complete accident. In the raging bull market of the late 1960s and early '70s, Warren couldn't find any more cheap stocks to buy, so instead of changing investment strategies, he closed down his partnership and cashed out of the game. Then came the crash of 1973–74, and Warren, loaded with cash, suddenly found all his favorite companies selling at bargain prices, and he bought like crazy. Charlie, with his investment partnership, had stayed in the game, and in the crash of 1973–74 lost half his investors' money—which he later recouped, but the crash was a traumatic event for him. The difference between the two was that when the crash came Charlie was sitting on a load of stocks that all went down, while Warren was sitting on a pile of cash and could buy stock in great companies at bargain prices.

Warren has said that this one event, being loaded with cash and waking up in the middle of the 1973–74 stock market crash, changed the whole course of his career. His "loaded for bear" cash strategy shows up most dramatically in the crash of 2008–9, when Warren, through Berkshire, became the lender of last resort for Goldman Sachs ($5 billion), Bank of America ($5 billion), Mars candy company ($6.5 billion), General Electric ($3 billion), Harley-Davidson ($300 million), and he picked up the entire BNSF Railway for $26 billion.

Charlie put the strategy into a little more practical terms: "*The way to get rich is to keep $10 million in your checking account in case a good deal comes along.*" Which, as we noted before, is the reason Berkshire is sitting on over two hundred billion dollars in its checking account, waiting for the next good deal to come along.

No. 55

"People cling to cash usually at the wrong times."[2]

＊

The stock market is at an all-time high, business is booming, the banks have never been stronger, people are buying everything—cars, new houses, second homes, art—and every investment they make is a winner. When everyone is spending like crazy is when Warren stops spending and starts hoarding cash.

The stock market is crashing, businesses are closing, the banks are failing, and people are hoarding their cash, and to get even more cash, they start selling things, like their investments, their real estate, and their stocks. In the process they drive stock prices into the ground. Prices haven't been this cheap since the Great Recession!!! When everyone starts hoarding cash is when Warren cracks open the vault and starts spending his cash hoard, buying the beaten-down stocks everybody else is desperate to sell.

In some ways, Warren's investment philosophy really is that simple.

No. 56

*"Cash is to a business as oxygen is to an individual:
never thought about when it is present, but it's the only
thing in mind when it is absent."*[3]

※

Commercial paper is unsecured short-term debt—with a maturity of one week to 270 days—that large corporations and financial institutions use to finance short-term obligations, like payroll, inventory, and seasonal expenses. One of the reasons they use this is that it carries a much lower interest rate than longer-term debt. Which is where the problem starts. Instead of putting long-term financing in place, some companies started using commercial paper to finance their long-term needs. The companies just kept rolling over their commercial paper when it came due—which worked very well until the financial crash of 2008 and the entire $2 trillion commercial paper market froze up. Nobody was willing to keep buying these companies' commercial paper, and suddenly companies didn't have any cash. Harley-Davidson was one of those companies, and by 2009 it was in real trouble and needed hundreds of millions in cash really quick. But no one would loan it to them. Warren came to Harley's rescue by having Berkshire loan it $300 million for five years at an annual interest rate of 15% ($45 million a year). When Warren was asked why he didn't just buy Harley-Davidson's stock, he replied, *"I kind of like a business where your customers tattoo your name on their chest, and I knew enough about the company to lend them money; but I didn't know enough to buy the stock."* Harley-Davidson survived, and Berkshire made a $225 million profit on its $300 million investment.

No. 57

"There will be some time in the next 100 years, and it may be tomorrow, and it may be 100 years from now, and nobody knows, where Berkshire cannot depend on anybody else to keep our own strength and to maintain our operations. And we spent too long building Berkshire to have that one moment destroy us."[4]

❋

Tucked away in the back of Berkshire Hathaway's 2023 10-K form, filed with the SEC, is a clause regarding stock repurchases that reads: "However, repurchases will not be made if they would reduce the total value of Berkshire's consolidated cash, cash equivalents and U.S. Treasury bill holdings below $30 billion." This is the fail-safe amount of cash Warren wants Berkshire to keep in its vaults at all times, to ensure that it survives no matter what economic upheavals or disasters rain down upon its businesses, even after he has long left his masterpiece of enterprise to another captain to steer it through the turbulent seas of commerce.

CHAPTER NINE

Warren Buffett on Benefiting from One's Mistakes

No. 58

"The triumphs in life are partly triumphs because you know that everything isn't going to be a triumph."[1]

✳

Warren goes on to say, *"You're going to make mistakes in life, there's no question about it . . . There's no way I'm going to make a lot of business and investment decisions without making some mistakes . . . If you played golf and you hit a hole in one on every hole, nobody would play golf, it's no fun . . . You've got to hit a few in the rough and then get out of the rough . . . That makes it interesting."* Warren hit one into the rough in 1987 with his $700 million investment in Salomon Brothers, a Wall Street investment bank that got into serious trouble with the government regulators and was about to be shut down. It was a huge mess of epic proportions, which required Warren to step in as the company's chairman and Charlie to run the audit committee. Warren fired several top people, brought in a new CEO, and convinced the government to let Salomon continue on. In the end, he triumphed, saving both Salomon Brothers and his $700 million investment.

No. 59

"I'd rather learn from other people's mistakes."[2]

✳

Experience is the best way to learn. However, it can be costly because of all the mistakes involved. When Thomas Edison was inventing the light bulb, he failed a thousand times before he got it right. You cannot afford many mistakes when investing.

Warren is a voracious reader of biographies—of people and businesses. Reading is where he discovered that he could learn from the mistakes of others, at an accelerated rate, and at the bargain price of the book. By simply picking up a book, Warren walked in the shoes of John D. Rockefeller as he built his financial empire. Watched J. P. Morgan courageously stop the stock market crash of 1907 that threatened the nation with economic ruin. And he was there with Thomas J. Watson Sr. as he struggled to build IBM. Not only did Warren study the successes, but he also studied the failures, as Wall Street is littered with vast fortunes both won and lost. Warren got an immense amount of worldly wisdom by reading a lot of books—most of which are available for free from any public library. And if they don't have the book you are looking for on their library shelves, a nice person behind the counter will be happy to get it for you through their interlibrary loan program. All for free!

No. 60

*"You can get in more trouble with a
good idea than a bad idea."*[3]

✳

Benjamin Graham taught that every good idea has limits. Not recognizing those limits is where things can go seriously astray. As Warren explains, *"People start off buying stocks because they think they are cheap—a good idea—but then they keep buying them as they go up and up, and before they know it, they are buying overpriced stocks—a bad idea—and that is when they get into trouble!"*

Warren will set a "price limit" when buying shares of a company he feels is underpriced. When that company's share price exceeds his "price limit," he stops buying, thus stopping his good idea from turning into a bad one. He recently did this with Apple—he kept buying over a period of several years, until Apple's stock hit a price he no longer found attractive.

No. 61

"A line from Bobby Bare's country song explains what can often happen with corporate acquisitions: 'I've never gone to bed with an ugly woman, but I've sure woke up with a few.'"[4]

❋

Warren has made a few mistakes over his career. One of the worst was the acquisition of the Dexter Shoe Company in 1993 for $433 million in Berkshire stock. When he bought Dexter it looked like a great company. He sang, *"There is no business like the shoe business."* Dexter's high-quality American-made shoes had a following—which created a kind of brand loyalty. And shoes are an absolutely necessary product. Americans buy a billion pairs of shoes a year that all eventually wear out, so people have to keep buying new ones.

What Warren didn't anticipate was that in the late 1990s cheap Chinese shoes would flood the American market and destroy Dexter's business model. Dexter's high labor costs in Maine couldn't compete with the cheap Chinese labor. Dexter still makes shoes, but the company is a fraction of the size it was when Warren bought it. When he was recently asked what his worst mistake was, he replied, Dexter Shoes. *"I gave away 1.6% of Berkshire—a wonderful business—to buy a worthless business . . . Dexter is the worst deal that I've ever done."*

No. 62

"After buying and supervising a great variety of businesses, Charlie and I have not learned how to solve difficult business problems. What we have learned is to avoid them."[5]

❋

There is an old saying in the real estate business that sometimes the best investment decision you can make is to say no. Charlie Munger, said it even better: *"The difference between a good business and a bad business is that good businesses throw up one easy decision after another. The bad businesses throw up painful decisions time after time."* And both Warren and Charlie learned this lesson the hard way with investments in a windmill manufacturer, a department store, a textile factory, a shoe manufacturer, and an airline. Why were those businesses bad? Because they were involved in highly competitive industries that beat each other up over price, which brought their profit margins down, killed their cash flow, and diminished their chances of long-term survivability. But Warren's and Charlie's business mistakes ended up a blessing. For they both learned that the secret to successful investing is to avoid the bad businesses and troubled industries and always to go with the better businesses that possess some kind of long-term durable competitive advantage—even if they must pay a fair price for it.

No. 63

*"We had a department store in Baltimore in 1966,
and if we'd kept it, we would have gone out of business.
So, recognizing reality is also important. I mean, you
do not want to try and fix something that's unfixable."*[6]

*

In 1966 Warren and Charlie bought 100% of a seventy-year-old, family-run, historically successful, brand-named downtown Baltimore department store, Hochschild Kohn, which sold high-quality merchandise, had superior customer service, and held the annual Toytown Parade, a much beloved Baltimore Thanksgiving tradition. Warren and Charlie thought they were acquiring an "old" established business, which they were getting at a considerable discount to book value. It seemed to be a bargain that had more than enough of a "margin of safety" to ensure them tremendous success. Great fortunes have been made in the department store business across America for the last hundred years. Warren and Charlie had both been raised in Omaha, where the Brandeis family had made a fortune in the department store business, and in 1966, they were still making money at it.

What Warren and Charlie didn't realize is that the new shopping malls in the suburbs were just beginning to take business away from the fabled department stores of yesterday. That was probably the reason the Hochschild and Kohn families were selling out; they could see the handwriting on the wall. Warren and Charlie quickly wised up to the fact that what they thought was an "old" established business was really a slowly dying one, and sold out in 1969 for about what they paid for it. Charlie later lamented, *"Buying Hochschild Kohn was like the story of a man who buys a yacht. His two happiest days are the day he buys it, and the day he sells it."*

CHAPTER TEN

Warren Buffett on Valuing a Company and Its Stock

No. 64

"Sooner or later, the amount of cash that a business can disgorge in the future governs the value it has in the market."[1]

✳

Warren's Wall Street mentor, Benjamin Graham, taught that over the short run the price on a company's stock is determined by a popularity contest—which can drive a companies' share prices down to insane lows and up to ridiculous highs. But over the long term the company's share price will reflect the "intrinsic value" of the cash the company will earn. Graham's strategy was to buy when a stock was insanely low and sell it when it rose up to its intrinsic value.

What Warren realized is that there are few companies that have a durable competitive advantage that have a gradual but ever-increasing value. Over the short term the stock market's "popularity contest" can undervalue them, but over the long term the stock market will eventually realize that ever-increasing value and revalue their share price upward. Warren also learned that if he acquired one of these wonderful businesses when the stock market undervalued it that it was far more profitable to hold it for the long term, letting its superior economics grow the business over a ten- or twenty-year period, than it was to simply follow Graham's strategy of selling the stock when it reached intrinsic value.

Charlie put it like this: *"If you buy something because it's undervalued, then you have to think about selling it when it approaches your calculation of its intrinsic value. That's hard. But, if you can buy a few great companies, that are ever-increasing in value, you can just sit on your ass."* This can best be seen with Berkshire Hathaway, which over the last fifty years has traded anywhere from below book value in

101

the early 1970s to almost twice book value in the late 1990s. If we had bought in at below book value and sold it at twice book value, we would have made great money. However, we would have missed the giant move Berkshire's stock made in the period from 2011 to 2024, when its class A shares increased from $104,000 a share to $632,000 a share. If we pick the right company, as Charlie says, it pays to sit on our ass.

No. 65

"The idea of projecting out extremely high growth rates for very long periods of time has caused investors to lose very, very large sums of money . . . Charlie and I will very seldom—virtually never—get up into high digits. You can lose a lot of money doing that."[2]

❋

Projecting out extremely high growth rates for very long periods of time produces crazy high valuations when discounted back to present value. If you use those high valuations to determine if a stock is a bargain or even fairly priced, you can be in for a very rude awakening down the road. Let us show you some of the dangers Warren is talking about.

Let's say a company has been growing its per share earnings for the last ten years at an average annual growth rate of 15% and its current 2024 earnings are $4 a share. If we project that 15% growth per share rate out for the next fifty years, we get per share earnings of $4,335 a share in 2074. Discounting to present value that $4,335 per share earnings—by using a discount rate of 5%—we get a discounted value of $378 a share, or 94 times the 2024 per share earnings of $4 a share. But if we change the projected period to twenty years, we get a projected value of $65.47 a share in year twenty, 2044. Discounting $65.47 a share to present value—using a 5% discount rate—we get a present value of $24.50 a share, or 6.1 times the 2024 per share earnings. The farther out—in terms of years—we push the growth rate, the higher the valuations get, and the higher they get, the more dangerous they are for us to use.

No. 66

"Book value is not a factor we consider,
future earnings is a factor we consider."[3]

❋

Warren got his start in the early 1950s investing when stocks were actually selling below their per share book value. He would look for stocks of companies that were selling at half their per share book value and buy them. He called it buying a dollar for fifty cents. And when the stock price rose up to book value, he would sell his shares, making a 100% return on his investment. But this kind of investing had limitations in that it did not take advantage of the ever-growing value that a company with a durable competitive advantage has, where the superior underlying economics of the business just keep on growing and growing, and adding more and more value to the company—value that Warren could only realize if he held the stock for twenty or more years.

Consider this: Warren personally spent approximately $6 million buying Berkshire Hathaway stock from 1965 to 1968, acquiring 394,754 shares for himself. If he had sold those shares when he first doubled his money, he would have made a 100% return on his investment. But he didn't sell them. He kept them. And Berkshire's stock price over the last fifty-nine years has risen from $12.50 a share in 1965 to over $632,000 a share in 2024, giving Warren a return of approximately 50,580 times his original 1965 investment. If Warren hadn't given so much of his Berkshire stock away to charitable foundations over the last thirty years, his original 394,754 shares would be worth approximately $249 billion today. Which would've made him by far the richest person on earth—even richer than the fabled entrepreneur Elon Musk. And none of this would've been possible if Warren had stuck to the "old way" of buying at half of per share book value and selling it later on for a 100% return on his investment. For Warren, future earnings are always where the big money is, which is why he is focused on the future and not on the past.

CHAPTER ELEVEN

Warren Buffett on Real Estate Investments

No. 67

"Under most conditions it is really
hard to find real estate that is mispriced."[1]

✳

Warren has never shown any interest in real estate investments, and
the reason for that is that it is an ultracompetitive market with many
sophisticated players who use large amounts of leverage. Because
of the large amounts of debt used to finance the deals, property
prices are largely dictated by mortgage interest rates, which means
that real estate is seldom, if ever, selling at bargain prices. Also, the
irrational panic selling that happens in the stock market, which
gives Warren his great buying opportunities, almost never happens
in real estate. Nor do real estate investments offer Warren the kinds
of returns he would find competitive with other investments in
his universe.

Consider this: The real estate capitalization rate (cap rate) is the
annual rate of return expected on the purchase price of a building.
The cap rate on a class A office building in New York City is cur-
rently 3.5% to 5%. By putting 30% down and financing the rest of
the purchase price, one can push the rate of return on the "down
payment" up to 6% to 10%. But that 6% to 10% rate of return will
be taxed in the current year, which would give the individual investor an after-tax rate of return of 3% to 5%. Warren has never found
those kinds of returns attractive.

However, Warren, having voiced his reluctance to invest in
real estate, has on occasion invested in several different real estate
investment trusts (REITs). REITs are essentially trusts that own and
manage a large number of commercial properties. Many REITs are

publicly traded. During economic upheavals, like 2008, they can become mispriced in relation to their payout. When this happens, Warren has been a buyer of a selective number of REITs that offer a payout that is attractively priced when compared to Treasury interest rates.

No. 68

"Anybody who goes into the real estate business is told the first rule, the second rule, and the third rule is never sign your name to anything."[2]

✳

There are many types of real estate loans. One of them is a non-recourse mortgage, where the bank's only recourse in the event of default is to seize the property itself. The bank can't go after the borrower. The bank cannot go after any of the borrower's other assets, such as their bank accounts, savings, or wages, to recoup the loan amount. Banks don't like issuing nonrecourse loans, but they will offer them to attract large real estate deals, provided the developer has an excellent credit history and can provide a substantial down payment to give the bank added protection in case the developer defaults on the loan. Real estate developers love nonrecourse mortgages because they can use their investors' money for the down payment, take out a $100 million nonrecourse mortgage, default on the loan, and then walk away scot-free, sticking their investors with the losses and the bank with the defaulted property. There's no business like the real estate business.

No. 69

"If you owe the bank $100, that's your problem.
If you owe the bank $100 million, that's the bank's problem."[3]

✳

This is where the investment philosophy of Warren Buffett and the reality of Donald Trump finally meet up. If a company defaults on a $1 million real estate loan, the banks are more than willing to foreclose on the $1 million property, sell it at a 20% loss, and write off the loss against the bank's current year's earnings. The bank is willing to do this because the $200K loss is a hit to the bank's earnings that it can easily absorb.

But if a company borrows $100 million to develop a building and then defaults on the loan, and the bank sells the property for a 20% loss, which equates to a $20 million loss, it could severely impact the bank's yearly earnings. Banks don't like having a negative $20 million "problem" on their books, so they try to avoid them like the plague. Which they often do, by renegotiating the loan package with the borrower—so the borrower can keep on developing the building—and the bank doesn't have to foreclose and take it back.

Trump experienced this "bank not wanting to foreclose" phenomenon when he owned the Plaza Hotel in New York City in the 1990s. The Plaza was losing money and Trump was in trouble on loans to several banks he borrowed from to buy the Plaza. The banks had to decide: To foreclose or not to foreclose? The banks chose not to foreclose, and instead they took a 49% ownership interest in the property, leaving Trump with 51% controlling interest. Why? Because the bank was not in the business of running a hotel; it didn't have the management talent for it. If they had foreclosed and kicked

Trump out, they might have had to shut the hotel down till they found another buyer. And an empty hotel is not worth as much as a hotel with guests in it. It was much better to have Trump keep running the Plaza until the property either turned itself around or it was sold.

CHAPTER TWELVE

Warren Buffett on the Dangers of Banking

No. 70

"A banker once told me, 'I don't know why we keep looking for new ways to lose money when the old ways of losing money were working so well.'"[1]

✳

Banks make money by running what is called a mismatched book—they borrow short-term, and they lend long-term. The bank pays depositors 3% to keep their money in the bank, which the depositor can withdraw at any time, and the bank then goes out and loans that money to a borrower at 5%, pocketing an annual 2% profit on the spread. This might not seem like much, but when you are talking billions of dollars in loans, 2% can add up quickly.

However, banks can also get hit for enormous losses if borrowers default on their loans. The real estate developer defaults on his $50 million nonrecourse loan—sticking the bank with millions in losses. If the bank's loan losses are large enough, the loss can wipe out the bank's equity, and the depositors' money. Because this "loan loss" scenario played out so many times in the early 1930s, with depositors losing all their money, the government stepped in and created a very peculiar mutual insurance company to protect depositors' money called the FDIC. (The FDIC currently protects depositors up to the amount of $250,000.)

What is odd about the FDIC is that it is run by the government, but it is actually financed by the banks themselves. The banks pay a yearly fee to the FDIC for insuring their depositors' bank balances up to $250,000. If in any given year the FDIC runs out of money, it just assesses an additional fee on its member banks to cover the shortfall. In the ninety years the FDIC has been insuring depositors' money, it has never once cost the government a single penny.

No. 71

"A lighted match can be turned into a conflagration, or it can be blown out."[2]

✳

This is Warren talking about the 2023 Silicon Valley banking crisis. Let us give you a little history: During the 2020 to 2021 period of super-low interest rates, the yield on one-year US Treasuries fell to less than 1% to 0.1%. This means $100 million invested in one-year Treasuries would earn $100,000 a year in interest. But the yield on ten-year US Treasuries fell to 0.7%, which means that $100 million invested in ten-year Treasuries would earn $700,000 a year. A number of banks decided they would "reach for yield" by buying ten-year Treasuries. It seemed safe; they're US Treasuries.

But in 2022, the Federal Reserve Bank started to raise interest rates, and the banks that held positions in these ten-year Treasuries started to lose money. (As the yield on the new ten-year Treasuries goes up, the value of the older lower-yield Treasuries goes down.) Some banks sold out their positions, taking the loss. But some banks didn't because they didn't want to show the loss on their income statements. They decided to keep their losing positions, hoping the rise in rates wouldn't go too high. But rates did go higher, and several of the banks that held on to their ten-year Treasuries started to look like they would become insolvent.

Depositors caught wind of the danger these banks were in and started pulling all their money out of them. Which was made super easy by online banking. The banks, needing to raise cash to meet their depositors' demands, sold their ten-year bonds at a deep loss, pushing several over the brink into insolvency. This caused even more panic, and people started pulling money out of a lot of smaller banks, even ones that weren't in trouble. Which put the entire financial system in danger of collapsing. Responding to the catastrophe that was about to happen, the United States government stepped in and said no matter what the size of the deposit, or who the depositor was, their deposit would be protected by the US government. Which stopped the run on the banks just in the nick of time. Uncle Sam blew out the match right before it could start a financial conflagration that might have taken down the entire United States banking system.

CHAPTER THIRTEEN

Warren Buffett on Investing in Japan, China, and the Rest of the World

No. 72

*"I certainly think investment principles do not stop at borders.
If I were investing in China, India, UK, or Germany—
I would apply exactly the same sort of principles."*[1]

✳

Warren went on to say, *"I would think of stocks as a small piece of a
business—investment fluctuations being there to benefit me, rather than
to hurt me—and focus my attention on businesses where I thought I
understood the competitive advantage they had—and what they would
look like in five or ten years."*

Oddly enough, worldwide human investment behavior remains
predominantly short-term focused no matter the language or the
culture. Every economy will experience bull markets where businesses become overpriced, and all experience bear markets and panic
sell-offs. All have a few businesses that have some kind of durable
competitive advantage working in their favor. All have businesses
that will experience booms and busts and are impossibly hard to
value. And every one of them will have shortsighted investment
professionals, who misprice businesses and create opportunities for
the long-term value investor practicing Warren's principles.

No. 73

"The Japanese investments were simple. There were five very substantial companies, understandable companies, paying decent dividends and repurchasing their shares, and where Berkshire could manage the currency risk by selling yen-denominated debt to finance the sale."[2]

❋

In 2021 Warren spent the Japanese yen equivalent of $6.7 billion to buy into five major Japanese "Sogo shosha" trading companies— Mitsui & Co., Ltd.; Mitsubishi Corporation; Itochu Corporation; Marubeni Corporation; and Sumitomo Corporation.

Because Japan is an island nation, with no natural resources of its own, it is completely reliant on importing many of the materials needed for manufacturing and everyday life. This includes cotton, oil, natural gas, steel, minerals, beef, and many foreign-made consumer and industrial products. Japanese trading companies facilitate the import of these materials and products with their own international offices and trading partners all over the world. They also export Japanese-made products to the rest of the world.

All five trading companies have a long history of growing their earnings and buying back their shares. But what really made them enticing investments is that they were all paying a dividend of around 2%, and Warren could borrow the yen equivalent of $6.7 billion in the Japanese yen bond market at an average interest rate of 0.6%— which means he was making 1.4% ($93.8 million) a year on the spread between the 2% dividend he was earning and the 0.6% interest he had to pay (2% − 0.6% = 1.4%). Since the trading companies' dividend payout is in yen, Warren can use the yen dividend payment to make the yen interest payments on the yen-denominated bonds. Thus, currency fluctuations between the dollar and the yen don't come into play until many years from now, when Warren sells the Japan investments and brings Berkshire's capital gains back home to the United States.

In late 2023 Berkshire announced that it was back in the Japanese bond market borrowing even more yen, pushing its total Japan/yen borrowings to the equivalent of $8.8 billion. Berkshire also announced it was increasing its stock positions in the five Japanese trading companies to approximately 9% of their total outstanding shares. In 2024, Warren reported Berkshire is already showing an $8 billion–plus profit on its investment in these five Japanese trading companies.

No. 74

"Efficiency is required over time in capitalism."[3]

⁕

Within a capitalist market economy, innovation creates new business opportunities, but once the initial competitive dust settles, the remaining competitors are locked in a battle of efficiency. Why? Because over time, efficiency means lower costs, and lower costs enhance the business's profitability, which increases its competitiveness, and over the long run, improves its chances of surviving in a highly competitive marketplace.

This competitive battle for efficiency stands out most starkly in the silicon chip industry that got its start in California's Silicon Valley, a hotbed of technological innovation. In the beginning early innovators like Fairchild Semiconductor dominated the silicon chip market. But as time went on, more and more competitors began to produce silicon chips. These different companies started to compete with each other by making the chips ever more efficient, cramming more and more transistors onto each chip. Then they started to compete by making their production methods more efficient, so they could lower production costs, so they could lower prices to make their chips more competitive in the marketplace. Then, again, in the search for efficiency, companies started shifting production out of the United States to countries with lower labor costs, like Japan, Korea, and Taiwan. Finally, the quest for efficiency has driven the silicon chip industry to become highly specialized, with companies like Intel and Samsung designing, manufacturing, and selling their own chips. Then you have companies like

NVIDIA, Qualcomm, and AMD designing and selling chips, but having them manufactured by foundries like TSME in Taiwan. In the world of competitive capitalism, Charles Darwin's theory of "survival of the fittest" could easily be rephrased as "survival of the most efficient."

No. 75

"You will find plenty of opportunities in China. Charlie would say you've got a better hunting ground in China than even a person with similar capital in the United States."[4]

✳

The United States, which has a GDP of $23.02 trillion, has between 6,000 and 7,000 publicly traded companies on its stock exchanges. China has a GDP of $17.7 trillion and has 7,679 individual publicly traded companies on the combined stock exchanges of mainland China and Hong Kong. Any way we look at it, China's vast number of publicly traded companies, combined with its strong economy, have essentially doubled Warren's happy hunting ground for future investments.

No. 76

"What China's done in the last 50 to 60 years is a total economic miracle. I never would've thought it could have happened. But the truth is they're as smart as we are, they've working as hard as we are, and they can have growth in the economy from a lower base that will exceed ours percentage-wise for a long time. China's destined for a fine economic future, just like we are."[5]

In 1990, America produced 27% of the world's manufactured products, and China produced 3%. Today China manufactures approximately 28% of the world's products—compared to 16% for the United States. China consumes 13% of the world's products—while America consumes around 20%. China is dependent on exports to keep its economic engine going—America is dependent on imports to keep its consumers happy. China has a trade surplus; America runs a trade deficit. China owns $868 billion worth of United States Treasuries; American owns less than $1 billion worth of Chinese sovereign bonds. America consumes between 15% and 20% of China's manufactured products. An economic war between the two countries would be devastating for both countries because their economies are so intertwined.

No. 77

"I think China and the United States are absolutely destined to be the superpowers beyond my great-grandchildren's lives. They will always be competitors in business, and in ideas, in all kinds of ways ... We have to make sure that competition doesn't get us to the point that we don't realize that the best world is one in which both the United States and China prosper."[6]

✳

Let's be honest about this, conflicts between the superpowers are unavoidable—it's in their nature. They'll compete in business, and in ideas, and in a hundred different ways, on a hundred different fronts. But the one place we don't want them competing is in a war. There is zero upside to it. Which is one of the beauties of free market capitalism; every business transaction is a negotiated reciprocal altruistic exchange—you get what you wanted—I get what I wanted—we both benefit. We do this every time we go into a store and buy something. These same kinds of transactions go on between Americans and Chinese—directly and indirectly—a million times a day and people in both countries prosper, which makes a lot of people on both sides smile.

Of course, there is that pesky trade deficit America has with China. The US exports $195 billion of goods and services to China each year, and China exports $562 billion in goods and services to America. Which means that America is running a trade deficit with China of $367 billion. But this trade deficit number is really very deceiving—because it doesn't include money American companies earn by actually doing business in China, through their Chinese subsidiaries.

Consider this: The American company Yum!Brands—which owns KFC, Pizza Hut, and Taco Bell—has over 14,102 operating restaurants in China, spread across 2,000 cities, which represents almost 70% of Yums global store count. The Chinese are wild about KFC fried chicken—KFC makes up 10,000 of Yum's restaurants in China. For Yum, the China market brings in approximately 40% of Yum's $7.04 billion in revenues. Yet, Yum's revenues in China are not used in the calculation of the trade deficit between the two countries. Why? Because the trade deficit mainly tracks physical goods that cross the two countries' borders. It doesn't include Yum's 10,000 KFC restaurants serving up Colonel Sanders's finest fried chicken to an estimated one-third of China's 1.4 billion people every year.

So, we'd like to leave this topic with these two final thoughts: (1) A 2020 report by Boston Consulting Group estimated that American companies earn around $410 billion in revenue from Yum-like direct sales in China. Which would pretty much wipe out the $367 million trade deficit America supposedly has with China. And (2) we Americans really do love our iPhones—which are assembled in China—great job, guys! And we truly hope that millions of Chinese continue to love KFC's delicious fried chicken as much as we do our iPhones! See, it's a win-win—only happy faces on both sides.

CHAPTER FOURTEEN

Warren Buffett on Cryptocurrencies and Gold as Investments

No. 78

"Cryptocurrencies are like rat poison squared."[1]

✳

Warren went on to say, *"Basically, cryptocurrencies have no underlying value, and they don't produce anything . . . I could own all the Bitcoin in the world and the only way I'm going to make any money on it is if I can get someone else to buy it from me . . . That it doesn't have any intrinsic business value doesn't stop people from wanting to play the roulette wheel . . . Cryptocurrencies will come to a bad ending."*

The US dollar is both a paper and an electronic digital currency. Digital money electronically flies around the world every day with just a click of a button. You use digital dollars every day when you pay with a debit or credit card.

In the United States, for most of the twentieth century, the paper US dollar was backed by gold. The American government printed dollars, and those dollars went overseas, and people around the world would cash their dollars in for American gold. Eventually the United States Treasury started to run out of gold. So, America stopped exchanging dollars for gold. Today, the only thing backing the dollar is the law that says dollars are legal tender to pay all debts in America. The fact that you can exchange your dollars for a new lawn mower at Walmart or a new car at the Subaru dealer is what gives your dollars value. And if you used a credit card to pay for the mower or write a check to pay for the car, you are using digital dollars.

On an international level, after World War II, American business so dominated the world that the US dollar became the de facto currency for international trade. Saudi Arabia prices its oil in dollars and it expects to be paid in digital dollars—that are transferred electronically between accounts at the Federal Reserve Bank.

Only two countries in the world—El Salvador and the Central African Republic—recognize a cryptocurrency as legal tender. In all the other countries in the world you have to convert cryptocurrency into the local currency to pay your hotel bill, buy an airplane ticket, or pay your taxes. The reality is, if you own a cryptocurrency, in order to spend it, you have to convert it into dollars or euros or some other currency, which means you have to sell it. You cannot put cryptocurrency in a traditional bank and earn interest on it. Its greatest utility is its quasi-anonymity—government regulatory authorities have a difficult time finding out who owns cryptocurrency. It is used to facilitate the kinds of commercial transactions that some people would rather be kept quiet. Cryptocurrency has no inherent economic value. Its only investment value is purely speculative—people gambling on whether the price—in dollars—will either go up or down. And when people speculate on something that has no inherent economic value, prices can go way, way up, and they can go way, way down—all the way to zero. The part of that equation that Warren doesn't like is the "zero."

No. 79

"Gold gets dug out of the ground in Africa, or someplace else. Then we melt it down, dig another hole, build a vault, and bury it again. Then we pay people to stand around guarding it. Anyone watching from Mars would be scratching their head."[2]

❋

Warren argues that if you own a farm or an apartment building you can rent it out. If you own stocks, you own a piece of businesses that earn money. If you have $100,000 in cash you can put it in a bank and earn interest on it. If you own gold, it is a non-income-producing asset. Your only hope of making money on it is if you can get someone to buy it from you in the future, for more than you paid for it. Warren has always thought that investing in hope is a really bad idea.

CHAPTER FIFTEEN

Warren Buffett on the Dangers of Using Leverage/Debt

No. 80

*"You really don't need leverage in this world much.
If you're smart, you're going to make a lot of money
without borrowing."* [1]

✳

Leverage is just another name for debt. The attraction of using leverage (debt) is that it allows hedge fund managers and investment banks to make even more money. Let's say an investment fund has $200 million of investors' money invested in stocks. It can then take that $200 million in stocks and get a bank to loan it another $200 million at 4% interest a year. So, the fund now has a total of $400 million to invest. If the fund has a good year and earns a 20% return on that $400 million it will have earned $80 million, less its $8 million interest charge, giving it a total return of $72 million. Now, here is the magic: A $72 million return on the investors $200 million gives them a 36% rate of return. Without the additional leverage, their return would have only been 20%. Of the $5.5 trillion that American investment funds manage, approximately $2.5 trillion is borrowed money.

But here is the danger: Using leverage not only can dramatically increase our gains when things go our way, it can also dramatically increase our losses if things turn against us. The investment banks use way more leverage than the hedge funds do. How much more? The fabled Wall Street investment bank Lehman Brothers had a 28-to-1 debt-to-equity ratio—$618 billion in debt—when it went under. When leveraged bets went their way, the bank's management team paid themselves hundreds of millions of dollars in bonuses. But when their fortunes turned against them, the massive amount of leverage wiped out $22 billion in shareholders' equity in a matter of days, which ended careers and forced the 158-year-old firm into bankruptcy.

Warren has always avoided using large amounts of leverage/debt with Berkshire. He has also avoided investing in companies that have high debt-to-equity ratios. The result is that Berkshire has left some very easy money on the table. But it also means Warren and Berkshire's shareholders all sleep better at night.

No. 81

"Both Charlie and I, probably, have seen some more high-IQ people—really extraordinarily high-IQ people— destroyed by leverage."[2]

✳

Here Warren is referring to the collapse of Long-Term Capital Management, which was a hedge fund set up by the famed Wall Street bond trader John Meriwether in the late 1990s. Meriwether, in 1994, brought together some of the smartest people from Wall Street and academia, including PhDs in mathematics and economics, several of whom were Nobel laureates. Those brilliant minds devised strategies for investing in bonds and derivatives using tremendous amounts of leverage/debt, which, when things went their way, would earn outrageous returns on their limited partners' invested equity capital.

Meriwether's team employed bond spreads to make money and, at the same time, protect LTCM's trades from downside risk. They measured the historical spread between very similar bonds—such as the yield spread between two-year Treasury bonds trading in January and March. If the spread between January and March Treasuries greatly decreased or increased in relation to its historical average, LTCM would buy one and sell the other, betting that at some time in the future the spread would close back up—which it always did because they were essentially the same bond, just different expiration dates.

Using this strategy, LTCM often made 1% or less on a trade. Which might not seem like much, but multiply 1% by the $124.5 billion in capital it was working with, and it amounts to a profit of $1.24 billion. Earn $1.24 billion a couple of times a year, and you start showing outrageous returns on the $4.7 billion investors had invested in LTCM. In the second year of operation Meriwether earned his investors a 43% return on their invested capital of $4.7 billion in LTCM; and he earned a 41% return the third year. But here is the danger of leverage: LTCM had $124.5 billion in capital, of which $4.7 billion was equity from investors/limited partners, and the other $119.8 billion was borrowed from the Wall Street banks. LTCM was a 26-to-1 debt-to-equity leveraged operation.

Why would any Wall Street bank loan that much money on so little equity? Because LTCM was also putting up the bonds it was buying as collateral. LTCM would buy $119.8 billion in bonds, and those bonds would be put up as collateral to support a $119.8 billion loan from the banks. Which is why it seemed safe for the banks to loan LTCM so much money on so little equity.

Everything went great for several years. LTCM literally minted money for its investors. But then, in the summer of 1998, the Russian government shocked the world by defaulting on its government debt, devaluing the ruble and declaring a moratorium on payment to foreign creditors all in the same week. This caused the bond market to panic, and LTCM's spreads all went in the wrong direction, causing the company to show a massive loss, far greater than its supporting equity capital of $4.7 billion. When that happened, the banks that had loaned LTCM a total of $119.8 billion wanted either (1) more collateral or (2) their money back, and LTCM had neither. Literally overnight, LTCM became insolvent. The Federal Reserve Bank of New York went in and organized a group of Wall Street banks to take control of LTCM, and its investors ended up losing the vast majority of their $4.7 billion investment.

Warren's wisdom here is that a combination of supersmart people and large amounts of leverage can come to a catastrophic end. We might add that the combination of people with just average intelligence, and large amounts of leverage, can also come to the same tragic ending.

No. 82

"There is no such thing as a 100 percent sure thing when investing. Thus, the use of leverage is dangerous. A string of wonderful numbers times zero will always equal zero. Don't count on getting rich twice."[3]

✳

This is Warren quoting Charlie, who agrees buying shares in a company with a durable competitive advantage working in its favor, in a down market, can dramatically increase one's chances of success, but knows that there is no 100% sure thing. Which is why the use of debt/leverage is dangerous, and absolutely idiotic if you are already rich. But it is a repetitive tragedy in the world of investing.

Leverage has taken down some of the giants in the game, like Lehman Brothers, Bear Stearns, Long-Term Capital Management, and Archegos Capital Management (the family office, run by Bill Hwang, was brought down in 2021 by Hwang's highly leveraged bets on a handful of technology stocks that turned south). If some of the brightest people ever to roam Wall Street have been destroyed using leverage, just think of the disastrous results it could potentially produce for the rest of us.

CHAPTER SIXTEEN

Warren Buffett on Living a Happier and More Productive Life

No. 83

"If you invest in yourself, no one can take it away from you."[1]

✳

Warren believes that the best investment for most people is to invest in their own abilities or their own business before they start investing in foreign exchange currencies, commodities, stocks, bonds, ETFs, and the like. One can easily lose money in the markets, and one can lose their job, but it's virtually impossible to lose your education, skills, or vocation.

No. 84

*"I did decide, fairly early in life, that my
favorite employer was myself."*[2]

✳

Warren has always been happily self-employed. When he was still
in grade school, he started selling Coca-Cola door to door for five
cents a bottle. So driven to make money he'd ride his bike down to
the racetrack to look for mistakenly discarded racing tickets that
might be worth a buck or two. He even created a horse racing tip
sheet called the "Stable-boy Selections," which he sold for $3 apiece.
With his racetrack savings he bought his first stock at eleven, three
shares of Cities Service preferred for $38.25 a share. By the time he
was fifteen, he was delivering *Washington Post* newspapers, making
over $175 per month. He also purchased a used pinball machine at
age seventeen and placed it in a local barbershop; he eventually had
a pinball empire of three machines and was earning $50 per week.
When Warren left for college in 1947, he had amassed a whopping
$9,800—which may not seem like much today, but back then, in
Omaha, it would've bought him a nice middle-class home and a
new car to go with it.

No. 85

*"If you learn to communicate better—through writing
and in person—you increase your value by at least 50%.
If you can't communicate—it's like winking at a girl
in the dark. Nothing happens."*[3]

❋

In Warren's early days he was petrified of public speaking. He said, "*I
was terrified . . . I'd throw up if I had to do it—so I took a Dale Carnegie
course on public speaking—it really changed my life.*" Warren keeps
his much-prized Dale Carnegie diploma framed on his office wall.

After Warren took Dale's course, he taught a night class at the
University of Nebraska so that he could practice his oratory skills.
Two of his early investors, Drs. Bill and Carol Angle, were in that
class, and they were so impressed with the young man that they gave
Warren $30,000 for his investment fund. After Warren closed down
his fund in the late 1960s, the Angles followed him into Berkshire
Hathaway. By 2010 their initial $30K investment had grown to be
worth more than $300 million in Berkshire stock. If the Angles
still own their Berkshire stock today, it would be worth well over a
billion dollars.

No. 86

*"The only way to get love is to be lovable. It's very
irritating if you have a lot of money. You'd like
to think you could write a check: 'I'll buy a million
dollars' worth of love.' But it doesn't work that way.
The more you give love away, the more you get."*[4]

❋

Warren has said that he had a very loving father and a somewhat
distant mother. But his first wife, Susie, was the Queen of Love.
She painted friends and family with affection. Their upper-middle-
class home in Omaha was an open door for just about anyone in
the neighborhood who wandered in. If you were having a bad day
you could stop by the Buffett house and she would greet you with
a smile loaded with warmth. It was Susie who taught Warren that
love truly begets love. And though she is no longer with us, Warren
continues to radiate the warmth and love that Susie shared with all.

And for the record, to this day, Warren still lives in the same
home where he and Susie lovingly raised their three kids.

No. 87

*"If you hang around with people who behave worse than you,
pretty soon you'll start being pulled in that direction."*[5]

✳

Warren is a big advocate of hanging out with people smarter than
yourself and having exceptional people for your heroes—they will
pull you up, not down. If you can't be friends with them, he says, *"Just
pick out the person you admire the most in life, and sit down and write
the reasons why you admire them . . . Nothing could be more simple than
to try and figure out what you find admirable and then decide that the
person you* really *would like to admire is* yourself. *And the only way
you're going to do it is to take on the qualities of other people you admire."*
The people Warren admired most in life were his stockbroker father,
Howard; the famous baseball player Ted Williams; and the Dean
of Wall Street, Benjamin Graham. Baseball taught Warren a love of
statistics, his father taught him about honesty and introduced him to
the stock market, and Graham taught him to make a fortune buying
undervalued businesses. Warren's been hitting home runs ever since.

No. 88

"If you find evidence that is contrary to what you already believe, write it down, or else your mind will block it out. People have a great resistance to new evidence."[6]

✳

The mind is an efficient biocomputer, and once it has come to a decision, is resistant to changing it. The biological reason for this is that if we are constantly changing our mind, we will never get anything done, which would ultimately be detrimental to our survival. Writing down the contrary information forces us to deal with it directly and sets up learning software that weighs the new against the old. Warren experienced this phenomenon when he shifted from the Graham mode of investing—buying companies at halved book value—and started making long-term investments in exceptional businesses that have some kind of durable competitive advantage. Warren really struggled with the change at first, but he had Charlie reciting the new mantra every time he turned around, and he finally got it.

No. 89

*"I've never known anybody who was basically kind who died
without friends, but I've known plenty of people with money
who died without friends, including their family."*[7]

＊

Warren likes to tell a story about Tom Murphy, who, as we mentioned
earlier, was CEO of Capital Cities Communications. Tom grew
Capital Cities from a single television station into a media empire
that eventually swallowed the much bigger American Broadcasting
Company, and then went on to merge with an even larger Disney.
Warren says that in all the years he worked with Tom, he never once
saw him do anything unkind. Tom always erred on the side of kindness. That was one of the secrets to his success. Warren took this to
heart and made kindness one of the secrets to his success in working
with others.

No. 90

*"You want to pick a spouse who is better than you are—
and hope they don't figure it out too fast!"*[8]

※

Warren went on to say: *"All joking aside . . . You want to associate
with people who are the kind of person you'd like to be. You'll move in
that direction, and the most important person by far in that respect is
your spouse. I can't overemphasize how important that is . . . marry
the right person. I'm serious about that. It will make more difference in
your life. It will change your aspirations, all kinds of things."* Not all of
us will do so well as to marry the right person. However, in Warren's
case, he got lucky. When he was twenty-one, Warren married Susan
Thompson, the lovely nineteen-year-old daughter of a local university professor. Warren had to borrow his aunt's car to take Susie
on their honeymoon. They went to Las Vegas and stayed at the
famed Flamingo Hotel & Casino, then run by a family friend from
Omaha by the name of Jackie Gaughan, who graciously comped the
newlyweds' stay. Warren, upon seeing all the well-dressed people
stupidly gamble their money away, when they knew the odds were
clearly against them, had an inspired moment, and pronounced
to his young bride, "We're going to be rich!" Warren often credits
Susie with helping him grow out of his 1950s crew-cut nerdiness
and into the worldly financial wizard he is today.

No. 91

"How do I define success . . . If the people who love you are the people you want to love you, you're a success . . . You can have all the money in the world, with hospitals and libraries named after you, but if no one cares about you, in my view, you aren't a success."[9]

✳

Warren was friendly with a woman in Omaha—Bella Eisenberg, a Polish Jew, who, as a teenager, survived the Nazi concentration camps. She told him one day that she was slow to make friends, because every time she meets someone, she asks herself, if they came for the Jews again, would this person hide me?

When Warren talks to groups of MBA students, he is occasionally asked how he defines success. He often replies with this story about Bella, and ends it by saying, *"If you have a lot of people in your life who would hide you, I'd say you're a success."*

No. 92

"The rich invest in time; the poor invest in money." [10]

❉

This quote has a certain Zen koan—paradoxical—quality about it. But it is actually quite simple. The rich have all the material things money can buy. What they don't have—and can't buy—is more time. So, they spend millions on private jets to avoid wasting time in a public airport. They hire expensive concierge physicians to look after them so they don't have to waste time in waiting rooms to get in to see their doctor, and with the hope they might get better medical care and live a little longer. The poor, on the other hand, are just trying to acquire as much money as they can. They invest their money in things they hope will make them more money. So that they, too, can become rich enough to be neurotic enough to start investing their money in getting more time.

No. 93

"At Salomon Brothers, virtually everybody was dissatisfied with what they were getting paid. And they were getting paid enormous amounts of money. They were disappointed because when they looked at what a coworker was making, if it was more, it drove them crazy."[11]

✳

Salomon Brothers was once one of the great Wall Street investment banks. In 1987 Warren and Charlie bought $700 million worth of Salomon convertible preferred stock that was paying an annual interest payment of 7%. In 1991, one of Salomon's bond traders, who was driven to make even more money—than the millions he was already getting paid—rigged the system in his favor, broke the law, and got caught. This almost took Salomon down. Warren and Charlie stepped in to run the firm. Warren actually became Salomon's chairman. What our two heroes found was a sea of dysfunctional envy. Everyone knew what the person next to them was getting paid, and if it was more, it drove them crazy, to the point that they took unnecessary trading risks, even breaking the law. Warren and Charlie believe that envy is the silliest of all the seven deadly sins, since envy makes one feel bad about themselves, while the other six—pride, greed, wrath, sloth, gluttony, and lust—all have the potential to put a smile on your face.

No. 94

"I've noticed that the real advantage to inherited wealth is that it enables one to hate so much more effectively. If you've inherited a tremendous amount of wealth and you're mad at your brother, or a cousin, you can hire lawyers and go after them. Where the rest of us just might snub them at Thanksgiving."[12]

✳

The problem is that when wealth is inherited, people don't have to suffer the pain and toil of working year after year to get there. Those who get rich through hard work are way less likely to indulge the steep legal costs of settling interfamily squabbles with lawsuits. Part of the reason those with "inherited wealth" are so litigious is that the inherited wealth often tends to strip them of the self-worth one earns from honest work, so they are always looking for ways to redeem themselves through some imaginary battle, which their lawyers, for a fee, will most willingly indulge. Also, people with a lot of inherited wealth tend to have no problem throwing money away. After all, it was free money to begin with. In contrast, people who became rich on their own know there are way better things to do with their money, like investing it, so they can become even richer.

No. 95

"The two things you can't buy are time and love ... And I've been very, very, very lucky in life, in being able to control my own time to an extreme degree. Charlie's always valued that, too. That's why we really wanted to have money, so we could do what we damn pleased in our lives." [13]

＊

Charlie Munger put it like this: *"Like Warren, I had a considerable passion to get rich, not because I wanted Ferraris—I wanted the independence. I desperately wanted it. I thought it was undignified to have to send invoices to other people. I don't know where I got that notion from, but I had it. I wanted to get rich so I could be independent, like Lord John Maynard Keynes."*

Lord John Maynard Keynes was a highly influential British aristocrat, philosopher, economist, and successful investor who lived from 1883 to 1946. He is widely considered one of the most important economists of the twentieth century, and "Keynesian Economics" continues to shape world economic policy even today. His book *The General Theory of Employment, Interest, and Money*, published in 1936, was a big influence on both Warren and Charlie.

No. 96

"Write your own obituary and then try and figure out how to live up to it."[14]

✳

Warren is actually serious about this. It's an intellectual exercise that is designed to get you to use your imagination to give yourself life goals to work toward. Every journey begins with an imagined destination. If you can't imagine something happening, it probably never will. But if you can imagine it, and are willing to put in the hard work to get there, all kinds of magical things can happen. Even a nerdy teenage kid delivering newspapers growing up to be the sixth richest person in the world.

CHAPTER SEVENTEEN

Warren Buffett on Some Things to Avoid and a Few of the Potential Dangers That Might Lay Ahead

No. 97

"Speculation is most dangerous when it looks the easiest."[1]

✳

In 1969 Warren realized that the stock market had gotten completely out of touch with reality and was valuing businesses at insanely high prices. Everyone was making super-easy money—just buy shares in a company and watch your investment go up.

Instead of changing his investment philosophy of buying undervalued businesses, Warren sold everything, closed his investment partnership, and put most of his money in cash. As we mentioned earlier, his friend Charlie Munger, who was also running an investment partnership, kept on investing, enjoying the dizzy ride up. Then came the 1973–74 stock market crash, and Munger lost half of his investors' money. Warren, who had sat patiently out of the market for several years, found himself in 1973 loaded with cash and stocks suddenly selling at ridiculously low prices. He said, *"I felt like a sex-starved man who suddenly woke up in the middle of a harem."*

No. 98

"Reaching for yield is very stupid, but it is very human."[2]

✳

Here Warren is talking about bond yields. Riskier bonds pay a higher yield to compensate for the higher chance of the bonds defaulting. If bonds default, you won't get your money back! As bond buyers reach for higher and higher yields, they take on more and more default risk. The safest five-year bonds you can buy are US Treasuries. Suppose Treasuries are paying 5%, but you want a higher rate, and five-year junk bonds are paying 10%. So, on a $100,000 bond, the five-year Treasuries are going to pay you $5,000 a year and you are 100% sure you are going to get your money back when you go to cash them in. The junk bonds are going to pay you $10,000 a year, but there is only a 60% chance you will get 100% of your money back when you go to cash them in. You can buy the junk bonds and get a higher yield, but you end up taking on a whole lot more default risk—which means you might lose your entire $100,000 investment. Warren doesn't think the additional yield of a junk bond is worth taking on the additional risk of losing your entire investment. Or as he likes to say, *"The first rule of investing is don't lose the money. And the second rule of an investing is don't forget the first rule."*

No. 99

"There's a great desire of the priesthood in finance to want to teach the things that they know and you don't know and that they spent a long time learning and that maybe requires a fair amount of mathematics. And it really has nothing to do with investment success."[3]

✳

The volume on the US options market is approximately 10.2 billion contracts a year. It has been estimated that between 80% to 90% of all option contracts end up worthless. Yet an enormous amount of academic energy is spent creating mathematical models and trying to improve those odds. The longest option contracts that exist are called LEAPS, which expire three years after they are written. Options don't work for Warren because there are no ten-year option contracts that he can buy or sell that would give him control of 400 million shares of Coca-Cola stock or 907 million shares of Apple stock. Nor is there any cost-effective way for an individual investor to take a ten-year position in Apple stock using options to control even a thousand shares. But there are hundreds of mathematical formulas for an investor to use to try and beat the odds that their option contracts won't expire worthless.

No. 100

"We don't think the probability, in any given year, is necessarily very high that derivatives will either lead to or greatly accentuate some financial trauma. But we do think the danger is there . . . I know the managements of some of the companies that have big derivative activities, and they do not have their minds around what is happening."[4]

✳

There are four major types of derivative contracts: options, commodity futures, interest rate futures, and swaps. The Bank for International Settlements estimates that the notional or face value of the world's derivatives market is $632 trillion. This is approximately six times as large as the world economy, which is approximately $105 trillion. And what is US bank exposure to this derivative risk? The total notional value of derivative contracts held by US banks in 2023 was $221.9 trillion—larger than the $109 trillion market cap of the entire world stock market, and larger than the entire $133 trillion value of the world bond market. And if you are a bank, here is the best part: That $632 trillion world derivatives market can be mind-numbingly complex and not well regulated in some parts of the world, which means the bank's traders can often rule the roost. In the US alone, commercial banks pocketed $42 billion in trading revenues in 2022, much of it from trading derivatives. Because derivative contracts are so complex, Warren feels very few people in government, in academia, or in the banks themselves fully appreciate all the potential dangers they present. This has caused Warren to label complex derivative contracts as potentially *"financial weapons of mass destruction."*

No. 101

"The world is flipping a coin every day as to whether people who can literally destroy the planet as we know it, will do it."[5]

❋

Here Warren is talking about the threat of nuclear destruction of the planet. Because of self-preservation and the threat of mutual destruction, he believes the odds are remote of this happening. However, there is still a chance, a small one, that something will eventually go astray, and someone, some nation, will launch a nuclear weapon against another nation. Or some terrorist cell gets ahold of a nuke and uses it. Also, against all odds, accidents do happen. And the more countries in the world that have nuclear weapons, the greater the odds of one being used. It's not a matter of if it can happen, it is really just a matter of enough flips of the coin before it does happen. And that should scare the hell out of all of us.

CHAPTER EIGHTEEN

Warren Buffett on Investing in Technology Companies

No. 102

"At Berkshire, we make no attempt to pick the few winners that will emerge from an ocean of unproven enterprises. We're not smart enough to do that, and we know it."[1]

✳

Do you remember the internet bubble in the late 1990s? When the internet was taking over the world? And any and every internet company was the new rage? Well, Warren didn't own a single one of those "internet" stocks. When asked why not, he told a story about the early days of the automobile industry—that in the first twenty years of the auto industry there were over 1,900 different American auto manufacturers, but today there are just three American auto manufacturers. Then he went on to say that out of all the thousands of new internet companies out there he simply wasn't smart enough to pick out the winners from the losers. Eighteen years later he looked at the winners and picked one—Apple—and in the beginning of 2024 he had a profit of approximately $145.8 billion on his Apple investment. Good things really do come to those who can wait.

No. 103

"Apple is a better business than any of our other businesses . . . People are paying $1,000 for an Apple iPhone and $35,000 for a second car—if they had to give up one or the other, they would give up the second car."[2]

✳

Warren sees Apple as a global company with multiple products that owns a piece of the consumers' minds. The economics of Apple's business added to Warren's enthusiasm for the company.

From 2012 to 2016 Apple grew its earnings from $1.59 a share to $2.08 a share, for a compounded annual growth rate of approximately 5%. With per share earnings of $2.08—and paying an average price of $34 a share—Warren could argue that he bought himself an "Apple equity bond" that earned an initial rate of return of 6.1% ($2.08 ÷ $34 = 6.1%) that was going to grow at an annual rate of 5%. Also, Apple had a net cash position of $143 billion and was aggressively buying back its shares. The enormous cash position told Warren that the company had been hugely successful, had plenty of money for new product development, and didn't need any debt financing. The share repurchases told him that Apple was going to increase Berkshire's ownership in the company year after year without Warren having to spend another dime. For Warren, all these things added up to Apple being a good buy at $34 a share, or 16 times per share earnings, and he went on to acquire 907 million Apple shares, which in 2024 he started selling when he felt that they had become overvalued.

No. 104

"I made the wrong decision on Google . . . It wasn't like what they were doing was a mystery to me. The mystery was how much competition would come along, and how effective they would be, and whether it would be a game where four or five companies were slugging it out without making as much money as they could if one company dominated."[3]

✳

Warren was very aware of Google before it went public. GEICO was spending a considerable sum of money pushing their web pages on Google's internet search engine. Also, the founders of Google—Larry Page and Sergey Brin—came to see Warren in Omaha to talk with him about taking their company public. Why Warren didn't invest in their company is because he wasn't sure what their competition would look like down the road. Remember, at one time there were multiple internet search engines fighting for consumers' eyes. Alta-Vista, Yahoo, MSN, and Google were all competing with each other at the time. Warren didn't know which one would win the race, and he didn't feel he could pick the winner, so he decided not to invest.

Google ended up winning the race and today it has a 92% share of the desktop search market and 83% of the mobile search market. It is the undisputed leader in the global internet search market. Its parent company, Alphabet Inc., owns YouTube, and 62% of internet users in the US access YouTube daily. Alphabet has a 25% return on equity, and it has been buying back its shares; both would appeal to Warren. It has $155 billion in cash and short-term investments—its debt is 17% of its cash position—which would also make Warren smile. And—this is super important—it is one of the strongest and most aggressive developers of computer-generated artificial intelligence in the world. If AI is the next big moneymaker, Alphabet will be a big player in the game. It's easy to argue that Alphabet has a durable competitive advantage in multiple markets. We think the only problem for Warren is the price of the stock. Alphabet trades at a P/E of 26, but if it ever came down to a P/E of around 16, there is a very good chance we would start seeing Alphabet in Berkshire's stock portfolio. With Warren it's always a two-step process:

1) the right company
2) at the right price. Alphabet is arguably the right company, now it is simply a matter of price.

No. 105

"We have got a big appetite for wind or solar . . . If someone walks in with a solar project tomorrow and it takes a billion dollars or three billion dollars, we're ready to do it . . . The more there is the better . . . We're turning Iowa into the wind power capital of the world, the Saudi Arabia of wind."[4]

✳

Berkshire Hathaway Energy (BHE) has 3,400 wind turbines in Iowa, serving 2.3 million homes with clean renewable energy, and in Nevada it produces enough solar energy to power over 1 million homes. The national average monthly residential electric bill is $133.21, while the BHE average bill is 17.04% less at $110.52 per month. BHE generates $26 billion a year in average operating revenue and $3.1 billion in pretax profits. What makes all this investment in renewable resources work for BHE is government tax credits. BHE has received close to $6 billion in income tax benefits on a net basis in the last three years alone, which has reduced its tax bill to zero for the last three years. For Warren there is no business like the renewable energy business!

No. 106

*"There won't be anything in AI that can replace the gene . . .
AI can change everything in the world, except how men think
and behave . . . I think it is extraordinary—but I don't know if
it will be beneficial."*[5]

＊

Alas, the last time science seriously let the genie out of the bottle
was with nuclear energy. And our great achievement with it was to
create enough nuclear bombs to destroy the world a hundred times
over. Humans and their brilliant inventions. Will artificial intelligence be any different? Elon Musk, one of the founders of OpenAI,
is scared to death by the darker prospects of AI and is lobbying
hard for government regulation. That worked well with nuclear
energy—thus all the bombs. What will most likely happen is that
AI will be militarized, and a kind of AI arms race will develop. AI
is the future of war. Albert Einstein once said, "As long as there are
sovereign nations possessing great power, war is inevitable." Thus is
the nature of man that not even AI can change.

What is odd about the development of AI, unlike nuclear energy,
is that it is not being developed by government scientists but rather
by private industry. With the biggest players being Alphabet (Google) and Microsoft (which is linked to OpenAI). Which means that
these two companies will probably be the two biggest economic
winners in the AI revolution that lies just ahead.

CHAPTER NINETEEN

Warren Buffett on Berkshire Hathaway's Business Dynamics and Future

No. 107

"In the end, Berkshire should prove itself over time . . .
and it deserves to be continued in its present form.
It has a lot of attributes that are maximized by being in
one entity, which people don't fully understand."[1]

✳

Berkshire Hathaway is technically a conglomerate holding company, but what Warren has really created is an enormous well-capitalized "Insurance Company," with seventy different domestic- and foreign-based insurance subsidiaries, whose assets are a little over $250 billion in cash and short-term Treasuries, $353 billion in stocks, and sixty-five wholly owned noninsurance businesses, which generate billions in income every year. Berkshire's insurance businesses can suffer a super-catastrophic loss—like a Category 5 hurricane hitting Florida—in any given year and Berkshire will still be profitable because of the billions in income produced by its wholly owned businesses. Berkshire also insures other insurance companies all over the world through its "reinsurance business." In 2007 Berkshire Hathaway's National Indemnity Company provided Lloyd's of London with a $7.2 billion reinsurance policy, and in 2017 Berkshire—through National Indemnity—reinsured $20 billion of AIG's long-tail liabilities.

In contrast, most other insurance companies, are heavily invested in fixed-income bonds and preferred stock, which actually lose real value to inflation. But because Berkshire owns a portfolio of exceptional businesses that have a durable competitive advantage, freedom to price, and low capital needs, its businesses actually increase in real value with inflation. This level of capitalization and number of noninsurance business holdings is unique in the world of insurance companies. And it gives Berkshire a long-term competitive advantage that no other insurance company in the world has. To put it more bluntly, Warren has turned Berkshire into a fortress of capital, with the financial means to withstand the wrath of the gods and still come out smelling like a rose.

No. 108

"Berkshire buys businesses with great managers in place.
We've seen those people perform for, in many cases, decades.
We've seen their record, and they come with the business.
Now, our job is not so much to select great managers,
because we do have this proven record that they come with.
Our job is to retain them."[2]

✳

Warren always says that if the business doesn't come with great management, he doesn't want it, because he can't go out and hire great managers, as they are simply too hard to come by. Warren will often write a check for hundreds of millions of dollars to a business owner/manager for their entire company. So why on earth would these newly minted multimillionaires want to keep on working? Because their entire self-worth and happiness is wrapped up in running "their" business. This is one of the reasons they sell their business to Warren instead of to a private equity firm or to a competitor. They sell out to Warren, get a fat check for millions, and then he lets them continue running "their" business like nothing has changed. One of his owners who continued to work after the sale of her company to Berkshire was Mrs. B of the Nebraska Furniture Mart, who stayed on until she was 103. Warren does have company managers send him a letter every other year telling him who he should have manage the company if they dropped dead at the cash register tomorrow. Other than that, it's their baby, till the world ends or the day they die.

No. 109

"The real thing is to repurchase shares only when you think you're doing it at a price where the remaining shareholders are worth more the moment after you repurchased it than they were the moment before."[3]

✳

Warren will buy back Berkshire's shares if he thinks it will add more value to the remaining shareholders, compared to the value (cash) they are giving up by buying back the shares. Imagine that you have four shareholders and the company they own has a book value of $4 million. So, each shareholder is arguably worth $1 million. Now, if the company buys out one shareholder for $1 million, the company would have three shareholders and a $3 million book value remaining, and the remaining shareholders would still be worth $1 million each. The buyout of the one shareholder added no value to the other three shareholders.

But if the company buys out one shareholder for $1.3 million, the company would have three shareholders and a $2.7 million book value remaining, and the remaining shareholders would each be worth $100,000 less. In this case, paying $300,000 more than the shareholder's book value of $1 million destroyed shareholder value for the remaining shareholders.

However, if the company buys out one shareholder for $700,000, the company will have three shareholders and a $3.3 million book value remaining, and the remaining shareholders would each be worth $100,000 more. In this case, paying $300,000 less than the shareholder's book value of $1 million added shareholder value for the remaining shareholders.

When Warren's investment partnership first acquired controlling interest in Berkshire back in 1965, Berkshire had 1,137,778 shares outstanding, and Warren's partnership controlled 54% of the company. Warren then used Berkshire stock buybacks and open market purchases over the next three years to give his partnership an even greater ownership interest in Berkshire. By the end of 1967 Berkshire had reduced its number of outstanding shares to 985,482 and increased Warren's partnership control to 69% of the company.

Regarding Berkshire's most recent share buybacks, Warren considers Berkshire's intrinsic value to be worth considerably more than its book value, so he is willing to pay more than per share book value, as long as he can buy it below Berkshire's per share intrinsic value. In 2018, Warren bought back Berkshire's shares at 146% of its per share book value, paying a price of $310,000 a share for Class A stock. In 2019, he bought back Berkshire's shares at 127% of its per share book value, paying a price of $333,000 a share for Class A stock. In 2020, he bought back Berkshire's shares at 119% of its per share book value, paying a price of $468,000 a share for Class A stock. In 2021, Warren bought back Berkshire's shares at 128% of its per share book value, paying a price of $439,000 a share for Class A stock. In 2022, he bought back Berkshire's shares at 144% of its per share book value, paying a price of $468,000 a share for Class A stock. (To determine per share book value, take the shareholders' equity value found on the balance sheet and divide it by the number of shares outstanding.) In each case he increased the value of the shareholders' equity.

No. 110

"Berkshire has one enormous advantage . . .
and that is, we have a system at Berkshire where we
can allocate capital without tax consequences."[4]

✳

See's Candies earns more than it can spend on its operations, so Warren used See's excess cash to help Berkshire buy the BNSF Railway. He also used some of See's excess cash to help Berkshire buy Apple stock. When Berkshire pulled the cash out of See's to use elsewhere, it did so without incurring any kind of transfer tax. Berkshire can do this with all of its wholly owned companies. It is able to allocate capital tax-free between its different companies. It can even use their cash tax-free to buy other companies. What adds to this tax advantage is that Berkshire owns dozens of niche businesses, which really don't have the ability to grow, so Warren can use their excess cash to buy other businesses. Most companies spend their excess cash trying to expand the existing operations or buying a competitor. It never occurs to them to take the excess cash and go buy a completely different, but better business.

Warren first did this with Berkshire Hathaway itself. In 1967 Berkshire was a struggling company in a slowly dying textile industry. Instead of reinvesting Berkshire's excess cash back into its textile business, Warren used it to buy the National Indemnity Company. Later, Warren would pull cash out of National Indemnity to buy the Nebraska Furniture Mart, which he pulled cash out of to buy Borsheims, which he pulled cash out of to help him buy Dairy Queen, which he pulled cash out of to help him buy the Acme Brick Company, which he pulled cash out of to help him buy Shaw

Industries (carpets). This process just kept on going, over and over again, till today, Berkshire owns sixty-seven different companies, which have a total of 260 different subsidiaries.

What stops other CEOs from reinvesting retained earnings in completely different businesses is that they are predisposed to stay in the business that they made all of their money in. The CEO of an oil company wants to buy another oil company, they don't want to buy a paint company, like Warren did when he bought Benjamin Moore.

Brickmakers are brickmakers, candymakers are candymakers, carpet makers are carpet makers, and never the three shall mix, unless they are bought by Warren. And his secret is that they remain separate operating companies even after Berkshire buys them, nor do their managers shift jobs from one company to the other. In many ways it's as if Berkshire never really bought their company, until Warren shows up to collect the excess cash they earn so he can use it to go buy another company, and another company, and another company . . . And that is how Warren grew Berkshire into the behemoth it is today.

No. 111

"Our country's future prosperity depends on having an efficient and well-maintained rail system. Conversely, America must grow and prosper for railroads to do well. Berkshire's $34 billion investment in BNSF Railroad is a huge bet on that company, and the railroad industry. Most important of all, it's an all-in wager on the economic future of the United States."[5]

✳

In 2009 Warren made Berkshire's biggest acquisition ever, the $34 billion purchase of the entire BNSF Railway Company. But why then? And why not before? The railroad industry for over a hundred years had been a highly competitive and capital-intensive one that wasn't very profitable. None of these qualities appealed to Warren and Charlie.

But over time things began to change in the railroad industry. Through the process of consolidation—one railroad buying another railroad—by 2009 there were five major railroad companies in America that controlled 80% of the national rail freight market. While no one railroad had a complete monopoly on the entire country, regional niches developed that created quasi-like monopolies. The BNSF came to dominate the Northwest, and, in the process, it became very profitable.

The BNSF Railway is the largest railroad in America by revenue—$23.8 billion in 2023; and the largest by route miles it controls—32,500 miles. The BNSF moves a ton of goods 470 miles on a single gallon of diesel. Your typical BNSF freight train replaces approximately 280 trucks on the road. And per ton-mile of freight moved, railroads emit far fewer dangerous emissions into the atmosphere than trucking. While still capital intensive, BNSF makes lots of money, and will do so for at least the next hundred years. And that is what appealed to Warren and Charlie when they pulled the trigger on this one.

No. 112

"We bought See's Candies for $25 million, and it's given us over $2 billion of pre-tax income, which we've used to buy other businesses. And if we tried to use all the retained earnings within the candy business, I think we'd have fallen on our face."[6]

＊

One of the early business lessons that Warren and Charlie learned is that some businesses work well within a small regional niche, but they have few if any opportunities to expand their operations beyond their niche. See's Candies is one of those businesses. See's is largely a West Coast operation, with 70% of its stores in California. Although there are stores in a few major cities, they were never successful in rolling stores out nationally. They finally came to the realization that instead of throwing good money after bad, it was smarter to use See's retained earnings to buy other businesses. Oddly enough many of the businesses they bought were also niche businesses that made lots of money but had little reinvestment opportunities. Niche businesses like Nebraska Furniture Mart and Borsheims were originally single-store operations that made Berkshire lots of money, which could be reinvested elsewhere. An interesting thing about these niche businesses is that, while they held a durable competitive advantage in their hometowns or states, because of limited growth potential, nobody wanted them, so they often sold at bargain prices compared to the businesses that did have growth potential. We should note that Nebraska Furniture Mart did eventually expand out of Omaha into several other cities, but this only happened when Berkshire started accumulating large amounts of excess cash in need of a home.

No. 113

"Berkshire did pay a dividend in 1967, $0.10 a share.
It was a terrible mistake. I went to the men's room and the
other directors voted for it while I was gone."[7]

✳

One of the "tools" of financial engineering that Warren uses to build shareholder value is the decision not to pay a dividend. Berkshire hasn't paid one since 1967. Dividends strip cash out of the business, which in some businesses might be the right thing to do, in that they make more money than they can use expanding their business and they aren't any good at finding other uses for shareholder money. But that is not the case with Warren. He has no problem finding other uses for Berkshire's retained earnings that add value to Berkshire, be it buying entire other businesses, investing in publicly traded stocks, or financing corporations in need. By never paying a dividend and retaining 100% of Berkshire's earnings and reinvesting them, Berkshire has added $500 billion–plus to shareholder's equity, and has seen its Class A share price rise from $20 a share in 1967 to $632,000 a share in 2024.

No. 114

"The test about whether to pay dividends or not is whether you can continue to create more than one dollar of stock market value for every dollar you retain."[8]

✳

Warren's dividend payout test is easy: On Berkshire's financial statement go to the "Consolidated Balance Sheet," then find "Shareholders' Equity," and under that you will find "Retained Earnings." This is the amount of after-tax earnings that Berkshire has retained in the business since it started. At the beginning of 2024 Berkshire reported total retained earnings of $607 billion.

The next step is to determine the market capitalization (Mkt Cap) of the company—to do this you take the number of shares outstanding and multiply them by the current market price of the stock. In Berkshire's case there are two classes of stock: 567,775 Class A shares with a total market value of $358 billion, and 1,310,561,508 Class B shares with a total market value of $546 billion, which gives Berkshire a total market capitalization of $904 billion ($358 billion + $546 billion = $904 billion). The Mkt Cap of Berkshire will change daily with the change in the price of both Class A and Class B shares.

Berkshire had total retained earnings of $607 billion, which has created $904 billion in market value for its stock. This means, for every $1 Berkshire retained, it created $1.48 in market value for its shares. According to Warren, under his dividend payout test, if Berkshire's Mkt Cap on its stock ever slips below its total "retained earnings," it would be time for Berkshire to begin contemplating paying out a dividend. Warren says, *"If the time comes when we don't think we can use the money effectively to create more than a dollar of market value per dollar retained, then it should be paid out."*

No. 115

*"I insist on a lot of time being spent, almost every day,
to just sit and think. That is very uncommon in American
business. I read and think. I do more reading and
thinking and make less impulsive decisions than most
people in business. I do it because I like this kind of life."*[9]

✳

Charlie Munger, Warren's partner for over sixty years, once described Warren's life as being almost monastic. As noted, Warren has lived in the same upper-middle-class house for sixty-five years. He has driven 1.8 miles every day to the same office for the last fifty years. He eats in the same restaurants, orders the same food, year after year. He doesn't own any mansions or expensive cars. He had a beach house in California when the kids were young, but sold it once they became adults. He does have a corporate jet to fly around in. But he drives himself to the airport. If you visited Warren in Omaha in his younger days, he more than likely would pick you up at the airport himself. He really only likes to do two things with his day: read a lot—like five hundred pages a day—and buy companies—lots of companies. And he has a war chest of over a $250 billion in cash to invest when he finds the right company.

Oh, we almost forgot, Warren also loves to play online bridge, and is a huge fan of Nebraska football—he never misses a game.

No. 116

"Berkshire without me is the same as with me,
I'm not much value added."[10]

※

Warren is humbly underestimating his influence as a guiding light and cohesive influence over the more than seventy operating companies he has assembled. But then again, there is a great deal of truth in his statement. The companies that he has acquired for Berkshire over the last fifty-nine years are all excellent businesses that have some kind of durable competitive advantage working in their favor, which gives them way-above-average operating results. Plus, the decentralized way that Warren has run Berkshire has created seventy very independent operating companies, with seventy very competent CEOs running them, some of whom Warren hasn't even spoken with in years. Which shows the level of trust he has in them. Berkshire may own these companies, but there isn't one of them that depends on Warren to keep their economic engine running at maximum rpm. So, if you own Berkshire stock when Warren finally passes—well after his hundredth birthday—our advice to you is this: Just sit back and continue to enjoy the ride!

No. 117

"After I'm gone, I believe the responsibility of capital allocation at Berkshire should be with Greg (Able). He understands businesses extremely well, and if you understand businesses, you understand investing in common stocks." [11]

✳

Greg Able is Warren's heir apparent, chosen by Buffett himself, to take the reins of Berkshire after Warren is no longer running the company. (We're thinking sometime well after he hits the century mark.)

Greg is a superior manager who has been CEO of Berkshire's energy division since 2008 and the vice chairman of Berkshire's noninsurance operations since January 2018. Greg's management skills are unquestionable. However, there has been concern among Berkshire shareholders about who will be making investment decisions after Warren has "retired." Here Warren is saying that Greg is the person he has chosen to make those investment decisions. If Greg simply follows Warren's tenets for investing—as we outlined in this book—Berkshire's shareholders have many more great years ahead of them.

No. 118

"We've got the money to buy in $100 billion worth of Berkshire's stock. If Berkshire's stock gets cheap, relative to its intrinsic value, we would not hesitate to spend $100 billion." [12]

❋

Berkshire Hathaway in the third quarter of 2024 had a little over $250 billion in cash, cash equivalents, and short-term Treasuries. Berkshire reported in 2022 that it will not repurchase its own stock if its cash cushion drops below $30 billion. Berkshire needs that $30 billion to comfortably operate its many businesses in even the darkest of times. This means that Berkshire could easily spend $100 billion or more on share buybacks if its stock started selling below its intrinsic value. We can argue—based on Berkshire's historic repurchases of its stock—that its intrinsic value is 20% to 30% north of the most Warren has paid for Berkshire stock in the past, which is 146% of its per share book value.

We will argue to you that one of the reasons for Berkshire's massive accumulation of over $250 billion in cash is that Warren is planning on making his last great bargain buy from the grave. When Warren passes on to that great stock market in the sky and the only way any of us can contact him is with a Ouija board—Berkshire's stock price probably will tank. And if Berkshire's stock price sinks below its intrinsic value, Berkshire's new CEO—channeling Warren—will launch the mother of all stock buybacks, potentially buying back 30% or more of Berkshire's shares. Which will make the remaining Berkshire shareholders—those who kept the faith—even richer.

CHAPTER TWENTY

Warren Buffett on Successfully Working with Other People in Business

No. 119

*"I like being trusted by people, I would rather do what
I do with partners than do it sitting in a room by myself,
even though I might make more money that way."*[1]

✳

Warren got his start investing other people's money and taking a cut of the profits. In the early days of the Buffett Partnership, he did something unheard of—he only took a fee if the partnership beat what investors could get from putting their money in a savings account, which was 4% back then. He ran the partnership from 1956 to 1969 and it never had a year it lost money. It had an average annual compounding rate of return of 29.5% before fees, and a 24.5% return after fees. And many of his early partners ended up his friends and fellow shareholders in Berkshire Hathaway. Today, Berkshire has over 3 million individual shareholders whom Warren refers to as his shareholder partners. And at the Berkshire annual meeting, for the last fifty-three years, Warren has spent up to six hours at a time answering individual questions from his shareholder partners. In Warren's mind, no matter how large Berkshire gets, it is still a partnership, and he is still their much-trusted managing partner.

No. 120

"Praise by name, criticize by category."[2]

※

The sweetest words anyone can ever hear are praise. The recipient will instantly like you. It's one of the easiest ways to make a friend. But nobody likes to hear criticism. Criticism is a quick way to make an enemy for life.

For Warren, who is managing dozens of CEOs from Berkshire's many companies, this has become almost a creed. He freely praises by name, but if he has to criticize, he will do it by category. On several occasions Warren has told the 20,000 Berkshire shareholders attending the Berkshire annual meeting that JPMorgan Chase's chairman and CEO—Jamie Dimon—is brilliant and one of the best in the banking business. But when talking about Wall Street investment banks during the 2008 financial crisis, he avoided saying anyone's name, and only said the bankers foolishly took on too much risk and did dumb things, which ended up taking down their banks.

No. 121

"You can always tell someone to go to hell tomorrow."[3]

※

This is actually some management wisdom that was given to Warren by Tom Murphy, head of Capital Cities Communications. You get pissed off at someone you work with and you tell them to go to hell, and suddenly you have to work with someone who is mad at you, and might stay mad at you for a very long time. Which doesn't make for a very pleasant work environment. The same thing happens with email and texting—your emotions get the better of you and before you know it you are whipping off a real zinger that you will probably regret in the morning. And you can't go back in time and erase it. Which brings to mind a similar bit of fatherly wisdom Warren shared with his three kids when they were growing up—he told them, *"It's easier to stay out of trouble than it is to get out of trouble."*

No. 122

"If you've got somebody working for you that lacks integrity,
you want them to be dumb and lazy."[4]

✳

Because if they are intelligent, energetic, hardworking, and creative, but lack integrity, the first four qualities are going to steal you blind. This bit of business folk wisdom was gifted to Warren early in his career by Peter Kiewit Jr., the chairman of the Kiewit Corporation, one of the largest construction companies in North America. Warren has leased his Omaha office, where Berkshire is headquartered, from the Kiewit Corporation since 1962. Kiewit was a guiding light to many in Omaha's business community, including Warren.

No. 123

*"You need to know how people manipulate other people
and you need to avoid the temptation to do it yourself."*[5]

✳

We won't try to teach you how people manipulate other people in
this book. But we can tell you the book that Warren and Charlie read
that taught them how people manipulate other people is *Influence:
The Psychology of Persuasion*. The author, Dr. Robert B. Cialdini,
spent his life studying and writing about persuasion. Read it and
learn how to spot someone who is using persuasion techniques to
manipulate you. But please take Warren's advice and try to avoid
using them yourself. You won't get very far in life if you are labeled
a manipulator who can't be trusted.

No. 124

"If you're going to spend eight hours a day working, the most important thing isn't how much money you make, it's how you feel during those eight hours, in terms of the people you're interacting with, and how interesting what you're doing is to you."[6]

✳

Think about it for a moment—the average person is awake 120 hours a week—if 40 of those hours are spent at work, we arguably are spending one-third of our awake adult life at our jobs. If we don't like the people we are working with, it can quickly turn into a really miserable life, even if we are making a whole lot of money.

Warren has always advised young people to pick the job they are interested in, and to work for people whom they respect and like. That way they will be excited about getting up in the morning and going to work, and they will enjoy it, and find it interesting. Which is the first step to living a happy and fulfilling life. But what about the money?

If one loves what they do, they are likely to rise to the top of their profession. Warren didn't make any money when he went to work for Benjamin Graham on Wall Street, but he loved what he was doing. Jeff Bezos started Amazon selling books out of his garage, working sixty hours a week and often slept at his desk, but he loved the problem-solving and creativity that came with building something that was completely new. J. K. Rowling was a single mother living on welfare when she was inspired to write *Harry Potter and the Philosopher's Stone*. If you work at something you love, the money will come. And if it doesn't, who cares, you're enjoying your work life—and how many people can say that?

No. 125

"The difference between successful people and really successful people is that really successful people say no to almost everything. You've got to keep control of your time, and you can't unless you say no. You can't let people set your agenda in life."[7]

❋

Success in any profession breeds demand, and often those demands come in the form of requests of your time. You're asked to join charitable boards, be involved in political causes, sit on oversight committees, give speeches, all of which take time away from the job, profession, activity that made you successful. For the passionate, like Warren, there is never enough time. For the bored, time is never ending. Really successful people never, ever have enough time, even when they learn to say no.

It is interesting to note that Apple's Steve Jobs had a very similar take on saying no. He said, "*People think focus means saying yes to the thing you've got to focus on. But that's not what it means at all. It means saying no to the hundred other good ideas that there are. You have to pick carefully. I'm actually as proud of the things we haven't done as the things we have done. Innovation is saying no to a thousand things.*"

No. 126

*"I think business culture has to come from the top,
it has to be consistent, it has to be part of written
communications, it has to be lived, and it has to be rewarded
when followed, and punished when not. And then it
takes a very, very long time to really become solid."*[8]

✳

What exactly is Berkshire's business culture? The main tenet of Berkshire's business culture is a deep commitment to decentralization. Berkshire's wholly owned operating companies function with remarkable autonomy. CEOs enjoy almost unfettered control over their respective businesses.

This approach stems from Buffett's belief that "trust" brings out the best in people. Warren views his CEOs as stewards rather than subordinates, which helps to unleash their entrepreneurial spirit. This lack of micromanagement allows Berkshire's many managers to freely tailor sales and production goals to directly respond to their markets.

Another piece of Berkshire's business culture is an unwavering commitment to ethical conduct. Warren once famously declared, *"Lose money for the firm and I will be understanding, lose a shred of reputation for the firm and I will be ruthless."* This ethos permeates every facet of Berkshire and its many companies, shaping interactions with customers, partners, and shareholders. Managers prioritize treating customers fairly, building enduring relationships based on mutual trust and transparency. This moral compass not only safeguards against reputational damage, but also builds customer satisfaction, which leads to repeat business and sustainable growth.

And finally, there is Berkshire's commitment to having a long-term perspective. Warren encourages Berkshire's CEOs to think years ahead, prioritizing enduring value creation over fleeting short-term profits. This frees managers from the shackles of quarterly pressures, allowing them to focus on innovation, employee development, and strategic acquisitions that might not yield immediate returns, and lay the groundwork for a more profitable tomorrow.

But make no mistake about it, every aspect of Berkshire's business culture is ultimately aimed at increasing shareholder wealth by adding long-term value to the company.

CHAPTER TWENTY-ONE

Warren Buffett on the Future of America and American Politics

No. 127

"Never bet against America."[1]

✳

Warren actually borrowed this from the famed Gilded Age Wall
Street financier J. P. Morgan, who, when asked how he got so rich,
replied, "I never bet against America." What is interesting is that this
investment strategy worked brilliantly for J. P. Morgan in 1890—he
liked buying stocks during market crashes—as it did for Warren 118
years later, who also likes to buy stocks during market crashes.

No. 128

"I don't think you need to worry about American ingenuity running out."[2]

✳

Warren went on to say, "*Our economy and our people, our system, has been remarkably ingenious in achieving the 160 million jobs we have now—when throughout the period ever since 1776, we've been figuring out ways to get rid of jobs.*" In 1820 there were 7.7 million people, or 79% of Americans, working on farms, feeding a population of 9.6 million. In 2023 there were 2.2 million people, or 1.3% of the American workforce, involved in farming, feeding a population of 334 million. If it wasn't for advances in technology and robotics (tractors, combines, etc.) America would need 260 million people working in farming to feed its population. We can argue that advancements in technology and robotics freed 258.8 million Americans from the toils of farming so they could do other things, like work on creating the Computer Mainframe Revolution (1940s–1960s), Minicomputer Revolution (1960s–1980s), Personal Computer Revolution (1970s–1990s), Mobile Computing Revolution (late 1990s–present), and Cloud Computing Revolution (2000s–present), where 2.2 million Americans work on server farms and in data centers, many of which are powered by electricity generated by Berkshire's renewable energy wind farms.

Even though many jobs are still tedious and boring, the best part of all these technological and robotic advancements is that Americans went from working seventy-two hours a week in 1820 to thirty-eight hours a week in 2023. Leaving them more time to enjoy their families, friends, and the amazing world we live in.

No. 129

*"We ought to do better by the people left behind,
by our capitalist system, but I don't think we
should kill the capitalist system, the golden goose that
has been laying golden eggs since 1776."*[3]

✳

Capitalism is the way that a civilization can allocate its energy and resources, using a market form of distribution in which people vote with their money on whether or not the business will succeed. Because of its very creative nature, capitalism has a destructive side to it. As new technology replaces old technology, new jobs are created as old jobs become obsolete and vanish. This works well until a manufacturing plant is shifted from one country to another country and people cannot follow the job. People who lose those jobs often find new ones, but many get left behind, as labor is not as internationally fluid as capital. Capital knows no national boundaries; it flows freely and quickly across borders, searching every corner of the earth for the highest return on investment it can find. Labor doesn't have this freedom. The person who loses their high-paying manufacturing job in Indiana to a new plant in China can't get up and move to China. Chinese immigration laws won't let that happen. They are stuck in America.

Historically, if nothing is done about the abuses of capitalism, they can lead to political unrest, centralized government planning, and nationalization of private business. Arguably it was the abuses of capitalism that helped spark the Russian revolution of 1917, China's communist revolution in 1949, and the Cuban revolution in 1959, all of which led to a communist form of economy replacing a capitalist system. In America and England, the failures of capitalism, and the suffering it caused, led to the gradual socialization of parts of their economies. For example, when America enacted Social Security in 1935 in response to the mass unemployment of the Great Depression. And when England nationalized its coal and steel industries and instigated free national health care in the period from 1945 to 1951.

But as Russia, and China, eventually learned, centralized government planning and nationalization of private business stifles the flow of capital to new innovative businesses, and leads to a backward approach to industry and commerce. This creates a lower standard of living compared to the capitalist world. Or as Warren's friend the U2 rock musician Bono once observed, "There's a funny moment when you realize that, as an activist: The off-ramp out of extreme poverty is commerce and entrepreneurial capitalism."

Warren truly believes that for the golden goose of capitalism to continue working its wonders for America, there needs to be a safety net for the American workers who get left behind. So they, too, can continue to share in the country's great wealth, even when their job for the last thirty years gets shipped off to China.

No. 130

*"I like to ask a candidate what are you for that
most of your followers are against."*[4]

※

This seems like some kind of trick question. But it isn't. It's Warren's way of discovering where the candidate's true passions lie. It also tells him the candidate's level of courage and conviction. Will the candidate give up votes for what they honestly believe in and show the personal strength to stand before the crowd and say, "*No*, we aren't going to do that. Even if it costs me the election"? Such personal conviction in a politician is a rare and beautiful thing.

No. 131

*"Over the years I've voted for both parties, but normally
I vote Democrat, however I'm not a card-carrying Democrat,
but I am a card-carrying capitalist."*[5]

❋

Warren's much-loved father was a die-hard Republican congressman
from Nebraska, and one would expect that he would follow in his
father's shoes, and he did for a while, but as he got older, and richer,
he found himself siding more and more with the Democrats on social
issues. Warren, being well aware that no candidate ever got elected
on just the billionaire vote alone, often joins his fellow capitalists
and votes for those who support American business, regardless of
their political affiliation.

No. 132

*"We live in a country, frankly, that is so good
that your children and grandchildren will
live a lot better than you live, even though an idiot
or two runs it from time to time in between."*[6]

✳

Please take comfort in this thought the next time an idiot wins a
presidential election.

No. 133

"The Declaration of Independence was an aspirational document—and we have made great headway in achieving those aspirations—but we still have a long way to go."[7]

*

When the Declaration of Independence was signed on July 4, 1776, women weren't allowed to vote, and the country had an old-world economic system that embraced chattel slavery. It wasn't until 1865 that slavery in America was finally abolished; and it took until 1920 for American women to get the vote. It wasn't until 1949 that Harvard let women attend law school—but it limited the number of women to thirty. It wasn't until 1969 that Harvard ended the quota. It wasn't until 1967 that the Supreme Court ruled that laws prohibiting interracial marriages were unconstitutional. But it took until the year 2000 for Alabama to finally repeal its laws on interracial marriages.

The first female CEO of a Fortune 500 company was Katharine Graham. In 1963 Graham—stepping in to fill the shoes of her late husband—became the CEO of the Washington Post Company. The first African American to become CEO of a Fortune 500 company was Dr. Clifton R. Wharton Jr., who, in 1987, assumed the roles of chairman and CEO at TIAA-CREF—a leading financial services provider for educators and other non-profit employees.

Warren lived through these historic moments, actively advocating for many of the social and economic changes that paved the way for such advancements. He personally tutored Katharine Graham on the complexities of Wall Street, helping to ensure her success.

And he has given away millions to support countless causes that have fought tirelessly for the realization of that noble American ideal, *"That all men are created equal, that they are endowed by their Creator with certain unalienable Rights, that among these are Life, Liberty and the pursuit of Happiness."*

Warren Buffett on Philanthropy

No. 134

"More than 99% of my wealth will go to philanthropy during my lifetime or at death . . . The reaction of my family and me to our extraordinary good fortune is not guilt, but rather gratitude." [1]

✳

Warren has donated billions of dollars to charity during his lifetime, already gifting more than half of his original shares of Berkshire Hathaway. Most recently, in June 2024, he converted approximately 900 Class A shares and more than 13 million Class B shares of Berkshire Hathaway stock. Approximately 9.3 million shares will be gifted to the Gates Foundation. The remaining shares will go to the four Buffett Family charities—the Susan Thompson Buffett Foundation, Sherwood Foundation, Howard G. Buffett Foundation, and NoVo Foundation.

In addition, over $500 million of Warren's wealth has been currently put to humanitarian use in war-damaged Ukraine by his son Howard, who has built a hospital and rehab center for civilian and soldier war amputees, spent $87 million removing land mines, financed a national lunch program for schoolkids so they can go back to school, spent tens of millions on replacing war-damaged farm equipment so farmers can get back to growing food, and so far has financed the replacement of over 120,000 bomb-smashed windows so people can return to their homes and live in them in the winter.

No. 135

"I like to think I can think outside the box, but I'm not sure if I can think outside the box when it's 6 feet below the surface and do a better job than three people who are on the surface who I trust completely."[2]

✳

In June 2024, Warren announced that when he finally passes on, his remaining fortune, estimated to be in excess of $130 billion, will go to one charitable trust, managed by his three adult children—Howard Buffett, Suzie Buffett, and Peter Buffett. The terms of the trust are such that all three must agree on any charitable disbursements the trust makes. This ensures that as time goes on there will be a Buffett running the trust as long as one of the three children is living. Warren's only instructions is the trust's billions *"should be used to help the people that haven't been as lucky as we have been."*

*

We sincerely hope that those of you who use Warren's teachings to obtain great wealth in life, will consider following him and his family in their passion for philanthropy and charitable work.

Best Wishes,

MB & DC

Acknowledgments

We wish to thank first and foremost our families—Erica, Nicole, and Sam; Kate, Dexter, and Miranda—for their infinite patience and love while we worked long hours on this book. We both owe a great debt of gratitude to our wonderful editors at Scribner, Rosalind Lippel and Colin Harrison, who skillfully shepherded us through the entire writing and editorial process. Mary owes a very special thank-you to her beloved sister, Laura SirMons, and her dear friend Christine Engelhardt. And last but not least, we both are eternally grateful for all the worldly investment wisdom that the much-loved Warren Buffett and Charlie Munger graciously shared over the many years with us and the rest of our fellow Berkshire Hathaway shareholders. They truly bestowed upon us all the gift that keeps on giving.

References

***

EPIGRAPH

1 https://www.insurancejournal.com/news/national/2023/11/29/749832
   .htm#:~:text=Under%20the%20heading%2C%20"Nothing%20
   Beats,might%20add%20bluntly—stated

CHAPTER ONE

1 https://www.youtube.com/watch?v=JvEas_zZ4fM
2 https://www.sarwa.co/blog/warren-buffett-quotes#:~:text="Do%20
   not%20take%20yearly%20results,belong%20to%20the%20short%20term
3 https://www.youtube.com/watch?v=uddpWu5-1Uk
4 https://www.youtube.com/watch?v=8OcegOGAGIs
5 https://finance.yahoo.com/news/warren-buffett-investment-advice
   -for-young-people-120219862.html
6 https://www.youtube.com/watch?v=JvEas_zZ4fM
7 https://markets.businessinsider.com/news/stocks/warren-buffett
   -25-best-quotes-berkshire-hathaway-annual-meeting-2020-5-1029160195
8 https://buffett.cnbc.com/video/2008/05/03/morning-session---2008
   -berkshire-hathaway-annual-meeting.html
9 https://buffett.cnbc.com/video/2008/05/03/morning-session---2008
   -berkshire-hathaway-annual-meeting.html; https://www.youtube.com
   /watch?v=OhIEqKIf7yU
10 https://www.goodreads.com/quotes/3240452-i-try-to-invest-in-businesses
   -that-are-so-wonderful

11   https://www.youtube.com/watch?v=JvEas_zZ4fM

12   https://www.fool.com/investing/general/2012/02/22/the-25-smartest
     -things-warren-buffett-ever-said-.aspx#:~:text=24.,speaks%20well%20
     to%20this%20statement

13   https://buffett.cnbc.com/video/2015/05/02/morning-session---2015
     -berkshire-hathaway-annual-meeting.html

CHAPTER TWO

1   https://buffett.cnbc.com/video/2004/05/01/morning-session---2004
    -berkshire-hathaway-annual-meeting.html; https://www.youtube.com
    /watch?v=63oF8BOMMB8

2   https://benlengerich.medium.com/why-warren-buffett-doesnt-invest
    -in-tech-companies-and-yet-his-largest-holding-is-apple-c0317a93979c#:~:
    text=Buffett%27s%20Strategy&text=The%20key%20to%20investing%20
    is,the%20durability%20of%20that%20advantage

3   https://benlengerich.medium.com/why-warren-buffett-doesnt-invest
    -in-tech-companies-and-yet-his-largest-holding-is-apple-c0317a93979c#:~:
    text=Buffett%27s%20Strategy&text=The%20key%20to%20investing%20
    is,the%20durability%20of%20that%20advantage

4   https://buffett.cnbc.com/video/2008/05/03/morning-session---2008
    -berkshire-hathaway-annual-meeting.html

5   https://buffett.cnbc.com/video/2018/05/05/morning-session---2018
    -berkshire-hathaway-annual-meeting.html

6   https://buffett.cnbc.com/video/2019/05/06/afternoon-session---2019
    -berkshire-hathaway-annual-meeting.html

CHAPTER THREE

1   https://www.youtube.com/watch?v=Tr6MMsoWAog

2   https://finance.yahoo.com/news/warren-buffett-best-quotes-154519517.html

3   https://barbarafriedbergpersonalfinance.com/saving-money-advice-warren
    -buffett/#:~:text=4.-,Use%20Debt%20Carefully%20and%20Limit%20
    What%20You%20Borrow,without%20borrowing%2C"%20Buffett%20says

4   https://pictureperfectportfolios.com/learning-from-warren-buffett-the
    -power-of-compound interest/#:~:text=Well%2C%20as%20we%20
    will%20see,lucky%20genes%2C%20and%20compound%20interest;
    https://givingpledge.org/pledger?pledgerId=177

5 https://buffett.cnbc.com/video/2008/05/03/morning-session---2008
-berkshire-hathaway-annual-meeting.html

6 https://buffett.cnbc.com/video/2023/05/08/morning-session---2023
-meeting.html

7 https://www.fool.com/investing/2023/04/17/worried-about-high-interest
-rates-heres-what-warre/

8 https://buffett.cnbc.com/video/2015/05/02/morning-session---2015
-berkshire-hathaway-annual-meeting.html

9 https://buffett.cnbc.com/video/2019/05/06/afternoon-session---2019
-berkshire-hathaway-annual-meeting.html; source of Munger quote: http://
www.quoteswise.com/charlie-munger-quotes-4.html

10 https://www.sarwa.co/blog/warren-buffett-quotes

11 https://buffett.cnbc.com/video/2008/05/03/morning-session---2008
-berkshire-hathaway-annual-meeting.html; https://www.analystforum.com
/t/what-does-this-quote-by-warren-buffett-mean/94756

CHAPTER FOUR

1 https://www.youtube.com/watch?v=Tr6MMsoWAog

2 https://www.ivey.uwo.ca/media/2809438/buffett-2008.pdf

3 https://www.fool.com/investing/2023/11/05/good-time-to-buy-stocks
-warren-buffetts-advice/#:~:text=When%20to%20buy%3A%20Buffett
%20believes,also%20learn%20from%20his%20actions

4 https://buffett.cnbc.com/video/2023/11/06/morning-session---1999
-berkshire-hathaway-annual-meeting.html

5 Both quotes: https://buffett.cnbc.com/video/2015/05/02/morning
-session---2015-berkshire-hathaway-annual-meeting.html

6 https://financhill.com/blog/investing/warren-buffett-bear-market
-quotes#:~:text=Losses%20aren%27t%20realized%20until,stock%20
market%20is%20manic%20depressive

7 https://buffett.cnbc.com/video/2022/05/02/morning-session---2022
-meeting.html

8 https://buffett.cnbc.com/video/2008/05/03/morning-session---2008
-berkshire-hathaway-annual-meeting.html#:~:text=We%20don%27t%20
think%20—%20what,run%20our%20eyes%20over%20them

9 https://sabercapitalmgt.com/1987-berkshire-letter-and-buffetts-thoughts
-on-high-roe/

10 https://buffett.cnbc.com/video/2008/05/03/morning-session---2008 -berkshire-hathaway-annual-meeting.html

CHAPTER FIVE

1 https://www.youtube.com/watch?v=UpGIJG02-Mw; https://www.you tube.com/watch?v=JvEas_zZ4fM
2 https://buffett.cnbc.com/video/2019/05/06/morning-session---2019 -berkshire-hathaway-annual-meeting.html
3 https://buffett.cnbc.com/video/2008/05/03/morning-session---2008 -berkshire-hathaway-annual-meeting.html
4 https://buffett.cnbc.com/video/2004/05/01/morning-session---2004 -berkshire-hathaway-annual-meeting.html
5 https://buffett.cnbc.com/video/2004/05/01/morning-session---2004 -berkshire-hathaway-annual-meeting.html
6 https://buffett.cnbc.com/video/2023/11/06/morning-session---1999 -berkshire-hathaway-annual-meeting.html

CHAPTER SIX

1 https://nymag.com/intelligencer/2008/09/warren_buffetts_dirty_words _of.html
2 https://buffett.cnbc.com/video/2004/05/01/morning-session---2004 -berkshire-hathaway-annual-meeting.html
3 https://quotefancy.com/quote/931542/Warren-Buffett-First-many-in-Wall -Street-a-community-in-which-quality-control-is-not
4 https://www.reuters.com/article/idUSKCN0XR0OO/
5 https://www.youtube.com/watch?v=8OcegOGAGIs

CHAPTER SEVEN

1 https://www.youtube.com/watch?v=JvEas_zZ4fM; https://buffett.cnbc .com/video/2008/05/03/morning-session---2008-berkshire-hathaway -annual-meeting.html
2 https://www.youtube.com/watch?v=joBnDqPfKfI

CHAPTER EIGHT

1 https://buffett.cnbc.com/video/2022/05/02/morning-session---2022 -meeting.html

2 https://buffett.cnbc.com/video/2014/05/03/morning-session---2014
-berkshire-hathaway-annual-meeting.html
3 https://www.azquotes.com/quote/1278019
4 https://buffett.cnbc.com/video/2014/05/03/morning-session---2014
-berkshire-hathaway-annual-meeting.html

CHAPTER NINE

1 https://www.cnbc.com/2019/04/29/warren-buffett-on-making-mistakes
-that-makes-it-interesting.html
2 https://www.youtube.com/watch?v=uddpWu5-1Uk
3 https://www.youtube.com/watch?v=JvEas_zZ4fM
4 https://nymag.com/intelligencer/2008/09/warren_buffetts_dirty_words
_of.html; https://markets.businessinsider.com/news/stocks/warren
-buffett-most-gruesome-mistake-dexter-shoe-9-billion-error-2020-1
-1028827359#:~:text=%22I%20gave%20away%201.6%25%20of%20a%20
wonderful%20business%20-%20one,Dexter%20Shoe%2C%22%20he%20
said
5 https://libquotes.com/warren-buffett/quote/lbr1w3m
6 https://buffett.cnbc.com/video/2019/05/06/morning-session---2019
-berkshire-hathaway-annual-meeting.html; https://www.valueinvesting
world.com/2014/07/berkshire-and-diversified-retailing.html

CHAPTER TEN

1 https://www.yapss.com/post/collection-warren-buffett-171-dot-com-bubble
-burst; https://www.gurufocus.com/news/970127/charlie-mungers-3-tips
-for-valuing-stocks
2 https://buffett.cnbc.com/video/2004/05/01/morning-session---2004
-berkshire-hathaway-annual-meeting.html
3 https://www.youtube.com/watch?v=a8Tw2Pm-zGU

CHAPTER ELEVEN

1 https://www.youtube.com/watch?v=gxK2vXKlFO8
2 https://www.youtube.com/watch?v=zTuOMVu9Kow
3 https://www.youtube.com/watch?v=zpPcx1BsxNE

CHAPTER TWELVE

1 https://www.youtube.com/watch?v=zpPcx1BsxNE
2 https://www.reuters.com/business/buffett-says-he-cannot-imagine-us-debt
-default-2023-05-06/#:~:text=%22A%20lighted%20match%20can%20
be,who%20do%20the%20wrong%20thing.%22

CHAPTER THIRTEEN

1 https://buffett.cnbc.com/video/2015/05/02/morning-session---2015
-berkshire-hathaway-annual-meeting.html
2 https://www.reuters.com/business/buffett-says-more-comfortable-with
-investments-japan-than-taiwan-2023-05-06/#:~:text=%22The%20
Japanese%20thing%20was%20simple,finance%20the%20sale%2C%20
he%20added
3 https://buffett.cnbc.com/video/2015/05/02/munger-efficiency-is
-required-over-time-in-capitalism.html
4 https://buffett.cnbc.com/video/2015/05/02/munger-efficiency-is-recovered
-over-time-in-capitalism.html
5 https://buffett.cnbc.com/video/2018/05/05/morning-session---2018
-berkshire-hathaway-annual-meeting.html
6 https://www.forbes.com/sites/miriamtuerk/2018/08/16/why-warren
-buffett-is-right-about-china/?sh=1da91ad41bff
7 https://www.youtube.com/watch?v=uddpWu5-1Uk

CHAPTER FOURTEEN

1 https://www.cnbctv18.com/business/bitcoin-was-probably-rat-poison
-squared-and-other-top-quotes-by-warren-buffett-14618511.htm#; https://
www.cnbc.com/2020/02/24/warren-buffett-cryptocurrency-has-no-value
.html#:~:text=Tech-,Warren%20Buffett%3A%20Cryptocurrency%20
%27has%20no%20value%27%20-%20%27I,own%20any%20and%20
never%20will%27&text=The%20Berkshire%20Hathaway%20CEO%20
and,in%20a%20Squawk%20Box%20interview; https://www.cnbc.com
/2022/04/30/warren-buffett-gives-his-most-expansive-explanation-for
-why-he-doesnt-believe-in-bitcoin.html; https://www.thestreet.com/crypto
/investing/warren-buffett-doesnt-mince-words-about-bitcoin; https://
www.investopedia.com/news/buffett-cryptocurrency-they-will-certainly

-come-bad-ending/#:~:text=%22In%20terms%20of%20cryptocurrencies%2C%20generally,s%20(MSFT)%20Bill%20Gates

2 https://www.goodreads.com/quotes/546212-gold-gets-dug-out-of-the-ground-in-africa-or

CHAPTER FIFTEEN

1 https://barbarafriedbergpersonalfinance.com/saving-money-advice-warren-buffett/#:~:text=4.-,Use%20Debt%20Carefully%20and%20Limit%20What%20You%20Borrow,without%20borrowing%2C%20Buffett%20says

2 https://buffett.cnbc.com/video/2019/05/06/morning-session---2019-berkshire-hathaway-annual-meeting.html

3 https://www.insurancejournal.com/news/national/2023/11/29/749832.htm

CHAPTER SIXTEEN

1 https://www.youtube.com/watch?v=Tr6MMsoWAog; https://buffett.cnbc.com/video/2005/04/30/the-best-investment-is-in-your-own-abilities.html

2 https://quotefancy.com/quote/931415/Warren-Buffett-My-idea-of-a-group-decision-is-to-look-in-the-mirror; https://buffett.cnbc.com/video/2016/04/30/morning-session—2016-berkshire-hathaway-annual-meeting.html

3 https://www.youtube.com/watch?v=Tr6MMsoWAog

4 https://markets.businessinsider.com/news/stocks/warren-buffett-25-best-quotes-berkshire-hathaway-annual-meeting-2020-5-1029160195

5 https://observer.com/2015/05/ive-followed-warren-buffett-for-decades-and-keep-coming-back-to-these-10-quotes/; https://www.inc.com/marcel-schwantes/warren-buffett-says-you-can-ruin-your-life-in-5-minutes-by-making-1-critical-mistake.html

6 https//www.youtube.com/watch?v=JvEas_

7 https://www.youtube.com/watch?v=4YYxAS4xeNM

8 https://www.youtube.com/watch?v=Tr6MMsoWAog; https://www.youtube.com/watch?v=KJcWrL4fQnk; https://www.cnbc.com/2018/05/14/warren-buffett-says-the-most-important-decision-is-who-you-marry.html; https://buffett.cnbc.com/video/2022/05/02/morning-session---2022-meeting.html

9 https://www.youtube.com/watch?v=yzuTj_t7ILs

10 https://www.azquotes.com/quote/536518#google_vignette

11 https://buffett.cnbc.com/video/2014/05/03/morning-session---2014
-berkshire-hathaway-annual-meeting.html; https://www.youtube.com
/watch?v=Ycd-Zel3ExM

12 https://www.google.com/search?client=safari&rls=en&q=warren+
buffett+on+envy&ie=UTF-8&oe=UTF-8#fpstate=ive&vld=cid:
f164d162,vid:-T3NanXhuxY,st:0

13 https://buffett.cnbc.com/video/2019/05/06/afternoon-session---2019
-berkshire-hathaway-annual-meeting.html; http://www.quoteswise.com
/charlie-munger-quotes-2.html

14 https://www.youtube.com/watch?v=4YYxAS4xeNM

CHAPTER SEVENTEEN

1 https://www.thestreet.com/investing/stocks/the-15-greatest-warren-buffett
-quotes-of-all-time-13207512; https://nymag.com/intelligencer/2008/09
/warren_buffetts_dirty_words_of.html

2 https://www.cnbc.com/video/2020/02/24/buffett-reaching-for
-yield-human-low-interest-rates.html; https://www.marketwatch.com
/picks/this-is-warren-buffetts-first-rule-about-investing-heres-what-to
-do-if-your-financial-adviser-breaks-that-rule-01635799738#:~:text=
Warren%20Buffett%20once%20said%2C%20"The,all%20the%20
rules%20there%20are

3 https://buffett.cnbc.com/video/2008/05/03/morning-session
---2008-berkshire-hathaway-annual-meeting.html

4 https://buffett.cnbc.com/video/2004/05/01/morning-session
---2004-berkshire-hathaway-annual-meeting.html; https://www
.investopedia.com/terms/d/derivativestimebomb.asp#:~:text=
Derivatives%20time%20bomb%20refers%20to%20the%20potential
%20for%20a%20dramatic,financial%20weapons%20of%20mass%20
destruction.%22

5 https://buffett.cnbc.com/video/2022/05/02/morning-session---2022
-meeting.html

CHAPTER EIGHTEEN

1 https://www.oldschoolvalue.com/stock-valuation/warren-buffett-valuation
-formula/#:~:text=Second%2C%20speculation%20is%20most%20
dangerous,that%2C%20and%20we%20know%20it

2 https://www.youtube.com/watch?v=UpGIJG02-Mw

3 https://buffett.cnbc.com/video/2018/05/05/afternoon-session---2018
-berkshire-hathaway-annual-meeting.html

4 https://www.cnbc.com/2017/05/06/warren-buffett-says-hes-got-a-big
-appetite-for-a-solar-or-wind-project.html; https://markets.business
insider.com/news/stocks/warren-buffett-berkshire-hathaway-invest-billions
-iowa-saudi-arabia-wind-2019-12-1028787852

5 https://www.youtube.com/watch?v=lGlpRe2WD6g; https://www.you
tube.com/watch?v=03sdWvFUg14

CHAPTER NINETEEN

1 https://buffett.cnbc.com/video/2019/05/06/afternoon-session---2019
-berkshire-hathaway-annual-meeting.html

2 https://buffett.cnbc.com/video/2008/05/03/morning-session
---2008-berkshire-hathaway-annual-meeting.html#:~:text=We%20
don%27t%20think%20—%20what,run%20our%20eyes%20over%20
them

3 https://buffett.cnbc.com/video/2019/05/06/morning-session---2019
-berkshire-hathaway-annual-meeting.html

4 https://buffett.cnbc.com/video/1994/04/25/afternoon-session
---1994-berkshire-hathaway-annual-meeting.html

5 https://www.cnbc.com/2009/11/17/warren-buffett-reasonable-return-is
-good-enough-for-longhaul-railroad-ride.html

6 https://buffett.cnbc.com/video/2019/05/06/afternoon-session---2019
-berkshire-hathaway-annual-meeting.html

7 https://buffett.cnbc.com/video/2023/05/08/morning-session---2023
-meeting.html

8 https://buffett.cnbc.com/video/2008/05/03/afternoon-session
---2008-berkshire-hathaway-annual-meeting.html

9 https://www.goodreads.com/quotes/432412-i-insist-on-a-lot-of-time
-being-spent-almost

10 https://www.youtube.com/watch?v=JvEas_zZ4fM

11 https://www.youtube.com/watch?v=BBXh2IveLm8

12 https://buffett.cnbc.com/video/2019/05/06/morning-session---2019
-berkshire-hathaway-annual-meeting.html

CHAPTER TWENTY

1 https://www.youtube.com/watch?v=xvAOaKJ8Meo
2 https://www.youtube.com/watch?v=4YYxAS4xeNM
3 https://www.youtube.com/watch?v=4YYxAS4xeNM; https://www.fool
 .com/investing/2020/01/07/10-lessons-from-warren-buffett.aspx
4 https://buffett.cnbc.com/video/2016/04/30/morning-session---2016
 -berkshire-hathaway-annual-meeting.html
5 https://www.youtube.com/watch?v=4YYxAS4xeNM
6 https://buffett.cnbc.com/video/2023/11/06/morning-session---1999
 -berkshire-hathaway-annual-meeting.html
7 https://ulm.edu/webguide/faculty/pdf/One-Important-And-Simple
 -Successful-Habit.pdf; https://www.inc.com/marcel-schwantes/warren
 -buffett-says-this-is-1-simple-habit-that-separates-successful-people-from
 -everyone-else.html
8 https://buffett.cnbc.com/video/2015/05/02/morning-session---2015
 -berkshire-hathaway-annual-meeting.html

CHAPTER TWENTY-ONE

1 https://www.youtube.com/watch?v=2RbGDN9HWO4
2 https://buffett.cnbc.com/video/2019/05/06/afternoon-session---2019
 -berkshire-hathaway-annual-meeting.html
3 https://www.youtube.com/watch?v=JvEas_zZ4fM; https://www.aei.org
 /economics/when-it-comes-to-reducing-global-poverty-bono-is-right-and
 -the-anti-capitalists-are-wrong/
4 https://www.youtube.com/watch?v=uddpWu5-1Uk
5 https://www.youtube.com/watch?v=uddpWu5-1Uk
6 https://buffett.cnbc.com/video/2008/05/03/morning-session---2008
 -berkshire-hathaway-annual-meeting.html
7 https://www.youtube.com/watch?v=2RbGDN9HWO4

AFTERWORD

1 https://givingpledge.org/pledger?pledgerId=177
2 https://www.wsj.com/finance/warren-buffett-gives-us-a-preview-of-his
 -will-419ad46d

Index

✳

bull markets, 37, 52, 55, 61, 165
as a "business market" versus "stock
    market," 53
common stock of amazing
    companies viewed as an Equity
    Bond, 9, 174
crashes of, 15, 85, 165, 211
decline of 1998, 47
financial crisis of 2008, 47, 200
gambling aspect of, 52, 53
global slowdown of 2016, 47, 65
higher the return, greater the risk, 72
holding shares, 11, 101–2, 104
letting the market serve you, not
    influence you, 55
a manic-depressive market, 50
outperforming cash, Treasury bills,
    and Treasury bonds, 10
predictions about, 46, 48, 71, 79
price versus value, 50–51
short-term trading as folly, 69
speculators and, 45, 165
steps for determining market value
    of a company and stock price, 3
stock market fluctuations and, 36
what the stock market is, 45
stocks: buying, 14
Buffett's basic investment
    principles, 31–42, 211
Buffett on, 17
buying big, 41, 85
buying into companies with a
    durable competitive advantage *at
    the right price*, 11, 21, 22, 23–24,
    25, 36, 41, 46, 47, 48, 51, 55, 97,
    176

"cigar butt approach," 21
considering a company's earnings, 4
emotions and, 17, 37, 50, 52, 55
good buy versus bad buy, 59, 60
Graham group's bi-yearly meeting,
    one stock to buy picked, 6
interpreting financial statements
    and spotting a bargain, 7
investing in companies with an
    increasing rate of return, 9
investing in idiotproof companies,
    13
knowing what you don't know, 32
listing companies to watch, 61
macroeconomic factors and, 49
mindset for: "I bought a business," 3
opportunity: bear markets, 21, 52,
    61, 65
opportunity: mispriced stock, 5, 52
opportunity: panic sell-offs, 16, 61,
    65, 69–70
opportunity: trouble-created price
    drops, 14–16, 36, 40, 46, 47, 64,
    211
"regardless of the price" bad buy, 61
the right price for buying, 59–65
setting a "price limit," 95
start-ups as risky, 5
"temperament" and "patience" for,
    14, 40, 41, 45, 46, 48, 52, 55
test of a good investment, 6
undervalued companies and, 32,
    101
Wall Street maxim about change, 5
when Buffett buys stock, 14, 16, 45,
    46, 47, 48, 50, 53, 64, 65, 87, 211

About This Book

*

To Buffettologists, Warren Buffett's aphorisms are more than simple statements of truth; they are akin to the teachings of a Chinese Taoist master, because the more you ponder them, the more they reveal the "path" or "way" to achieving great wealth. This collection of Buffett quotations and interpretations has specifically been selected to help you discover the "way" by taking you deep into the enlightened thinking of the greatest investor and philanthropist of our time. It is the authors' hope that the wisdom contained herein will help enrich your life by making your world a far more profitable, and a more enjoyable, place to live and work.

About the Authors

✳

Mary Buffett and David Clark have written ten bestselling books on Warren Buffett's investment methods. These books have been published worldwide in numerous languages.